What an incredible book! *Our I*
down. The captivation was not
love of my life," but, I found, these authors somehow knew me and my relationship with Taylor as if they had spent hours interviewing me. They know that remembering is the essential part of both grieving and healing and what better way to remember than to reach down into your deepest self and be creative. While most of us are certainly not poets, it is clear that does not matter. What does matter is that we own those key emotional words, thoughts, and expressions that are tied to our lost relationship. They are in us. The therapy comes when we invest the time to find them and make them sing what our soul is trying to say. We are the only ones that can tap those expressions and that kick starts healing. This expression starts something else also: our meager attempt at writing a poem about our incredible relationship ignites, enrichens, and somehow enlivens what we thought was gone. Those very words, from deep within us, are our undefinable connection with our sweet animal life that left us, holding only their collar, far too soon. There is no better way to grieve, heal, and honor their life. I cannot thank Drs. Louis Hoffman, Michael Moats, and Tom Greening, enough.

Jim Humphries, DVM
Veterinarian, Home with Dignity

Our Last Walk is a collection of poems that tells the story of the unconditional love and companionship our pets offer. It also shares the depth of the love and the grief that emerges for family members when a pet is suffering. Take a moment to sit down and read these heart-opening poems. This poetry reveals the soul connection between people and the pets that become family members.

Terri Goslin-Jones, PhD
Creativity Studies Specialization Lead and Faculty
Saybrook University

Our Last Walk will strengthen those struggling with the death of a beloved pet, in original verse written by those who truly understand what it means to love, grieve, and honor the lives of our animal companions. The poems in these pages are thoughtful, heartfelt tributes to the creatures whose days are always too brief but so beautiful in passing.

Gary Kowalski
Author, *Goodbye, Friend: Healing Wisdom for Anyone Who Has Ever Lost a Pet* & *The Soul of Animals*

This remarkable treasury gives words to the unspeakable grief and pain that so many of us feel when a beloved animal companion dies. It celebrates the special bonds we share with these wondrous loved ones. These poets give us the comfort of knowing that others understand what we are going through when we risk opening ourselves up to loving these fellow creatures and enduring the unendurable pain of losing them.

Kenneth S. Pope, PhD, ABPP
Co-author of *Ethics in Psychotherapy & Counseling, A Practical Guide* (5th ed.) and *How to Survive and Thrive as a Therapist: Information, Ideas, and Resources for Psychologists in Practice*

As a veterinarian, I see pet owners dealing with grief daily. Saying goodbye to a pet never gets easier, whether it is your first or fifty-first experience. It is important to take care of our pets as they near the end of their lives, but we must take care of ourselves, too. As a pet owner, we may find ourselves dealing with the shock of a sudden passing or the heart heavy task of deciding if and when the tie to end suffering is upon us and our pet. Dealing with grief is personal, difficult, and unique for each of us. Poetry allows us to relate to others who have experienced the loss of a pet as well as a venue for you own self-expression and healing. Using poetry to honor a pet's distinct personality not only serves as a tribute to our friends, but also as an avenue of healing and expression for ourselves. With the use of book, my wish for you, the reader, is to find a healthy venue for expression, peace in your heart, and satisfaction in knowing that you made a huge difference in the life of an animal.

Sean E. Snyder, DVM
Veterinarian, Parkway Veterinary Clinic

Our Last Walk:
Using Poetry for Grieving & Remembering Our Pets

Louis Hoffman, PhD
Michael Moats, PsyD
Tom Greening, PhD
Editors

Colorado Springs, CO
www.universityprofessorspress.com

Our Last Walk: Using Poetry for Remembering and Grieving Our Pets
By Louis Hoffman, Michael Moats, and Tom Greening

First published in 2016. University Professors Press. United States.

ISBN: 978-1-939686-15-2

University Professors Press
Colorado Springs, CO
www.universityprofessorspress.com

Front Photo by Lakoda Hoffman
Cover Design by Laura Ross

Dedication

For Amaya, a dog who taught me much about life, love, and relationships. You were never just a dog. You were a companion, a teacher, my comforter, a frequent inspiration, a friend, and part of our family. I still miss you.

~ Louis Hoffman

Poetry, Healing, and Growth Series

Stay Awhile: Poetic Narratives on Multiculturalism and Diversity
Louis Hoffman & Nathaniel Granger, Jr. (Eds.)

Capturing Shadows: Poetic Encounters Along the Path of Grief and Loss
Louis Hoffman & Michael Moats (Eds.)

Journey of the Wounded Soul: Poetic Companions for Spiritual Struggles
Louis Hoffman & Steve Fehl (Eds.)

Our Last Walk: Using Poetry for Grieving and Remembering Our Pets
Louis Hoffman, Michael Moats, and Tom Greening (Eds.)

Poems For and About Elders (Revised & Expanded Edition)
Tom Greening

Poetry, Healing, and Growth Series

Poetry is an ancient healing art used across cultures for thousands of years. In the Poetry, Healing, and Growth book series, the healing and growth-facilitating nature of poetry is explored in depth through books of poetry and scholarship, as well as through practical guides on how to use poetry in the service of healing and growth. Poetry written with an intention to transform suffering into an artistic encounter is often different in process and style from poetry written for art's sake. This series offers engagement with the poetic greats and literary approaches to poetry while also embracing the beauty of fresh, poetic starts and encouraging readers to embark upon their own journey with poetry. Whether you are an advanced poet, avid consumer, or novice to poetry, we are confident you will find something to inspire your thinking on your personal path toward healing and growth.

Table of Contents

Acknowledgments

We first would like to thank the many contributors to this volume. As we read through the poems, we were often drawn to tears. It is a blessing to have so many wonderful poets and pet lovers join us in this book. We would like to thank Dave Elkins, a friend and colleague to each of us, for agreeing to write a Preface. Dave is a wonderful scholar, sensitive clinician and friend, beautiful writer and speaker, and a pet lover. We have all shared many poems and pet stories over the years, and could not imagine anyone better to write a Preface for this book.

We would also like to thank all those who love their companions we call pets and who have shared their stories with us over the years. These have served as part of the inspiration for compiling this collection.

With each book, there are so many that I (Louis) feel I must acknowledge. To write or edit a book is a huge commitment, and often a huge sacrifice. I thank my wife, Heatherlyn, for tolerating my obsession with writing and supporting me in these many writing projects. I also want to thank my sons: Lakoda, Lukaya, and Lyon. I try to keep my writing from impacting time with you, but I know this is not always possible. I love you all very much. I also thank my parents, Clarence and Lynn, along with my brother and sister-in-law, John and Joy Hoffman, for their consistent support of me and my writing.

Amaya, to whom this book is dedicated, was my first dog. I never knew I could love a dog so much, but am thankful for this lesson that she taught me, as well as for so many other lessons. Dante, who was named after Dante's *Divine Comedy*, is also an inspiration for this book. As we began working on this volume, I worried he would not make it through the winter and began preparing myself for his death. I am thankful for the blessing of more time. Yet, as we finish up the book we are again faced with the scenario that his time remaining is limited.

East Springs Animal Hospital in Colorado Springs—all the doctors we have worked with, but especially Brad Bush, DVM—has always provided wonderful care for our dogs. I am deeply appreciative for their expert and sensitive care.

I decided to get Amaya when living with my graduate school roommate, Brad Robison, who supported this purchase and taught me much about being a dog owner. I am grateful. Brittany Garrett-Bowser is a fellow dog lover and someone who always supported my writing and my return to writing poetry. Several colleagues at Saybrook University—including Steve Pritzker, Theopia Jackson, Joel Federman, Stanley Krippner, and many others—have been wonderful supports at Saybrook and consistently encouraging of my writing. Several friends—including Shawn Rubin, Glen Moriarty, Richard Bargdill, Nathaniel Granger, Jr., Kirk Schneider, Ed Mendelowitz, and many more—have always encouraged and supported me in my career and writing. Thank you.

Special thanks goes to my co-editors, Michael Moats and Tom Greening. The idea for this book emerged from a presentation at the Existential Humanistic Institute (EHI) Conference in San Francisco in 2015. As we shared our love for dogs and poetry and our painful losses of pets, the idea for this book emerged. Tom has been an influential person in my life in many ways, including supporting my coming to teach at Saybrook University where I had the great privilege to teach alongside Tom for a number of years before his retirement. I feel deeply blessed by our friendship, Tom, as well as your support and the years we have been able to work together. Michael is a good friend who humorously, if generally graciously, tolerates the many ideas for projects, presentations, and books that seem to be constant in my consciousness. I am deeply blessed by and grateful for our friendship.

Pets have been a part of my (Michael) life since I was about six years old. Jake, a loveable little puppy, was my first dog and my first experience of losing a pet. The loss was not fair in the eyes of a six-year-old, yet it did not stop my love for dogs. Lady, a small beagle, was with me from elementary school through my sophomore year, and we faced some tough struggles together. There have been others that were phenomenal friends, including my ol' girl who ran free of this earth two years ago. These animals provided confidentiality, love, and trust at times when no one else could provide them all at once and with unwavering consistency. I would never miss the chance to have walked this earth with them even if it meant I could miss the pain of their deaths. It is because of our journeys that I find such a need for this book and understand how it can be a companion to those who are in the midst of their loss.

To compile this book with a group of pet lovers is an honor and a combination of joy, reflection, and shared pain. They share their encounters with grief and fond reflections of their dogs, their cats, and even their horses. It was important to allow their varied voices to reach out across the void in a manner that feels like a discussion with a friend—something important to each of the editors. I am thankful to be editing this project with Louis and Tom because of my appreciation for both of these men and what they have contributed to the field of psychology, for their love for poetry, and for the relationship they have offered.

As always, I am deeply appreciative for my wife, Annie, and her support in my creative endeavors. During the times when I sit silently and reflect, she patiently understands that it is an important part of my processing, my refueling, and my growth. She is my number one fan, and every article, poem, chapter, and book contains a piece of her.

Preface

David N. Elkins

If it's crazy to grieve over the loss of a beloved pet then count me among those who are stark raving mad.

Warning: The poems in this book may break your heart ... open. When I was asked to write the preface for this book, I felt honored. To prepare, I read a prepublication copy of the book that the editors had sent me. As I read the poems about grief, loss, and love, I was deeply moved. The poems hurt. They went straight to my soul and they hurt with a pain that has no balm. I thought of Peanuts, our little Yorkie. He's now 15 years old and is both blind and deaf. I know the day will come when we lose him. I have images of what it will be like when he's gone. I see his empty collar, the leash against which he once strained with excitement, his favorite toys, the ones he often laid at my feet to invite me to stop working and to play. One day, these will be the only material things we have to remind us of a pet who was so much more than a pet. We got Peanuts when he was nine weeks old. Foolishly, we thought we were getting a dog when, in reality, we were getting a member of the family. Although he's now old, blind, and deaf, he's still very much alive. He still wags his tail, kisses my nose, twists his little body with joy, rolls over in my lap for his daily belly rub, eats like a horse, and insists on going to the park for a walk every day at 5:30 p.m. sharp. Recently, I saw an announcement in our local newspaper about a priest who had set aside a day to bless pets. I liked the priest immediately because he recognized the specialness, even the sacredness, of pets. But I wanted to tell the priest that he had it backwards. We don't bless pets; they bless us.

According to an old myth, when the world was first created, humans and animals lived together as one. Then the gods decided to divide the world into human and animal. However, as the world was splitting in two, the dog jumped across the breach to spend eternity with humans. I like that myth, but I think it's too narrow. I believe cats jumped across too, as did horses, sheep, goats, pigs, cows, and all other animals. In fact, there is no breach; the world is not divided into human and animal. There's just one world and all of us, humans and animals, share it with one another. The boundary between humans and animals was invented by humans as a defense against the guilt we would otherwise feel for the way we use and abuse animals. If we make animals "other," then we can use, abuse, kill, and even eat them with little or no guilt. We can tell ourselves, "After all, they're just animals." Maybe one day we will no longer believe in false boundaries. Maybe one day we will no longer use and abuse animals for personal and corporate gain. Maybe one day we will abolish all exploitation of animals. Maybe we will extend compassion and respect to all animals, as we now do with our pets. The fact that we can love our pets gives hope for the human species. It says that we have the potential to extend compassion to all sentient beings and respect their right to inhabit the earth without being used and abused for our own selfish ends.

The poems in this book are written by kind, caring people who have opened their hearts to love an animal and to allow an animal to love them. As you read the poems, I hope you will open your heart and let them in. I believe the poems will move you. I suspect they will make you cry. They may touch your soul and cause your heart to hurt. However, if you stay with the process and not run away, you may find that the poems and the pain are transformative. You may find that the very poems that broke your heart have also opened your heart… to deeper respect and compassion for "all creatures, great and small."

Introduction: Grieving and Remembering with Poetry

Until one has loved an animal, a part of one's soul remains unawakened.
~ Anatole France

If you are reading this book, you are likely very aware of the beauty and joy that pets can add to one's life. Yet, with that beauty comes the inevitable loss when a pet dies. The deeper we love, the harder it is to say goodbye. Out of this paradox, along with many stories and shared tears, emerged the idea for this book.

The book was written for those who have lost a beloved pet as well as those who are journeying with others struggling with the loss of a pet. If you are reading because of your own loss, we hope that you may find healing and comfort in knowing you are not alone. If you are reading this because you are consoling someone who has lost a beloved pet, we hope the book will help you understand their pain and deepen your empathy for their loss.

The Invalidation of Pet Loss

In contemporary times, many people no longer have time or tolerance for grieving. Grief is often thought of as something to quickly "get over" (Hoffman & Moats, 2015), preferably out of sight of those who may be uncomfortable with your grieving. Indeed, there seems to be an increasing trend in our society, including in professional mental health organizations, to pathologize grieving if it is not resolved within a short amount of time.

This may be particularly true of those grieving from the loss of a pet. Pet owners often hear things such as, "It was just a dog" or "It was just a cat." Experiencing such invalidations, which frequently come from family members and close friends, intensifies the feelings of loneliness that can be part of the grieving process. Invalidations of this nature are prominent in the poems in *Our Last Walk*, such as Lisa Vallejos's poem, "Just a Dog." Vallejos's poem starts simply,

> They say "it's only a dog"
> I wonder if they have ever
> Had "only a dog"
> Like mine

But something shifts in the next lines,

> Her name is Dori
> I brought her home

This is a subtle shift, but poignant. Naming her and bringing her into one's home suggests an intimacy that is missed by those who say "it's only a dog." The poem goes on to tell the story of how Dori was part of her family. For pet lovers, their animals are members of their family who play particular roles and contribute to their family dynamics.

In the poem, "I Never Wanted to Say Goodbye," this theme is prominent as Hoffman, in his dog's last moments, writes,

> So many times I heard you were just a dog
> But tonight more than ever
> I wanted you to know
> I never believed that lie.

In these words, there is even a hint of anger at those who could not see that Amaya, his beloved companion, was not just a dog in the same way that a person is not just a friend or just a family member.

The anger can also be seen in Lac's poem, "The Love of a Childless Mother." Lac speaks of her experience of not having children and being told, though maybe not directly, that her love is not as real or valid because she has not known what it is to love a child as a mother. Many of the invalidations pet owners hear about their love may not be explicit, but they are clear nonetheless in implying that it is a lesser love. They are clear in not recognizing the grief for a pet as a real grief. They are clear in missing the depth of the pain that one is experiencing.

These invalidations are common to pet lovers. Anyone who has known grief knows that it can be a lonely experience. Often, the one we would most like to comfort us in that moment of pain is the one who is no longer there.

In many transitions in my (Louis) life, Amaya was the one who was always there. Early in our relationship I noticed that when I was sad, she would not want to leave my side. She followed me from room to room and was my most consistent comforter. While there were others in my life who were compassionate, caring, and supported me in difficult times, none were always there. The night that Amaya died, she was the one for whom I longed to comfort me in my pain. It was not just that she died, but that she could no longer comfort me and be there for me when I needed her most.

In the series of poems about Amaya in the second half of *Our Last Walk,* it is no wonder that two of the poems have themes of Amaya returning to provide consolation. Amaya became my symbol of comfort—embodying it. In my dreams, in my thoughts, in my poems, memories and images of her would emerge when I thought of comfort.

"Just a dog," just a cat," "just a horse," are words that are nonsensical to the pet lover. They can only be uttered by someone who has not done the work to understand, to be truly empathetic. These are words that strike a chord of pain and anger. They are words that demonstrate why books like *Our Last Walk* are needed.

Just Get Another Pet

One of the first questions often received after a beloved pet dies is, "Will you get another...?" Such questions, while good-intentioned, are similar to the statements, "Time heals everything" and "He/she is in a better place now." These messages are often received as being told that it is not okay to grieve, or that the beloved pet is replaceable.

But pets are not replaceable. In the poem, "Still Missing You," Hoffman writes

> You could not, would not
> Be a possession
> You fought to be something more
> And you won

Similarly, Gary Kowalski (2012), who has written extensively on pet loss, states,

> I use the term *owner* with hesitation. We may be the legal custodians of our animal companions and be responsible for their well-being, but while animals may be many things—cantankerous, humorous, neurotic, or supremely sane—they are never merely property. (p. 14)

Pet lovers know that while we may fall in love with another animal and invite them to join our family, this is not a replacement for the lost pet. We cannot simply replace a pet as we replace a book or phone or computer. Our pets have a personality and meet our needs in different ways.

When my (Louis) dog, Amaya, died, we were left with our other dog, Dante. While I love Dante, he could never be Amaya. Amaya was a very sensitive, intelligent dog. We developed a language to communicate beyond what I previously believed a dog and human were capable of. She was also very supportive and loving. While she shared her compassion freely with many when they were sad, her primary relationship focus was on our family. Dante, however, is a very different dog. He is very social and loves attention. When entering the veterinary clinic, he will howl and carry on until everyone gives him a proper greeting. But while he is very social, he is not a sensitive dog in the same way Amaya was. Amaya seemed drawn to people when they were sad and would just stay with them. Dante, on the other hand, will just want to play. After Amaya's death, I would often get frustrated with Dante because he was not more like Amaya. He did not provide the same type of comfort that Amaya did. Yet, I gradually accepted no dog could ever replace Amaya. As I let go of this expectation, Dante and I developed a much better relationship, and I began to appreciate Dante for himself. He may never comfort me the way Amaya did, but he excelled at cheering me up in other ways. His therapy was play therapy.

For some, the loss of pets is just too painful to consider trying to replace them. The poem "Making Iced Tea" begins with the lines,

> *I refuse to have any more animals,* he said.
> *I can't take the pain of letting go.*

Often, statements such as this are a stage in the grieving process, but for some they endure. When we invite a pet into our family, there is an awareness that the pet will likely die before we do. We are inviting the eventuality of death and grieving into our lives. In the midst of our pain and loss, it is hard to imagine inviting that pain back into our lives. Yet, if we can stay with the pain and explore it more deeply, we recognize that it is connected to much beauty in our lives as well. The pain of grief is part of the love and blessing that the pet has brought to our lives.

Paradox of Grieving

The inseparable connection between loving and grieving a pet is part of the paradox of grieving. Love inevitably brings with it pain and suffering; however, if we try to avoid love in order to avoid pain our lives quickly become bland.

Embracing the paradox of grieving can be an important part of the healing process. Healing in this context does not indicate a return to the prior state. When we encounter an important loss, this will stay with us for the rest of our lives, and we will never be the same for having endured it. We will always be grieving, but the grieving will change over time.

The poem "The Visit" concludes with the lines,

And thankfully
I am still
Missing you

This may seem like an odd statement. Why would one be thankful that they are still grieving? It is not thankfulness that one is still hurting, but rather the result of a recognition that the hurt is connected to the love (see also "Reflections on Poems for Amaya").

The subtitle to *Our Last Walk* is rooted in the recognition of this paradox: *Using Poetry for Grieving and Remembering Our Pets.* Remembering is part of the grieving process: remembering the pet, remembering the love, remembering what the pet added to one's life, remembering the pain. All this is intertwined. When someone grieving a pet tries to get through the pain quickly or tries to avoid or deny the pain, this often complicates the grief. Embracing the pain is part of the healing (Hoffman & Moats, 2015).

It Is Okay to Grieve

In the previous sections, there is an implicit message, "It's okay to grieve." These sections could even be read as fighting for the right to grieve. Grieving is something that is natural, but many feel as if they have to defend their right to grieve, especially when the grief is connected to a pet.

The poem "Let Me Grieve" addresses this fight. In the final stanza, Lac states,

> Don't tell me to be strong
> or say I'll be okay
> I know this to be true
> And still I hate goodbyes...

Then the poem concludes,

> But for now, let me grieve
> in order that I may survive.

In this poem, Lac shows an understanding of the wisdom of grieving. Grieving is not something we do, but something we need. Grieving is a very natural process. While cultures around the world have very different rituals and traditions around grieving, what is central is that these rituals and traditions exist. Throughout history and across cultures, there is a recognition of the need to grieve and have a process for grieving.

Unfortunately, it is common in contemporary culture for us to try to overcome our humanness and our limitations. As part of this, there seems to be attempts to cure or shorten the grieving process. Many are disconnected from their culture's grieving rituals and traditions, and these have not been replaced with new ones. Instead, many who are grieving are offered medications or other quick fixes that impede the natural grieving process. Grief does not magically disappear; it is something that we learn to live with. As we learn to live with grief, we change the way we experience it. It is no longer experienced as great a burden. We can begin to see the paradox of grieving: grief is connected to a blessing that is connected to what we are grieving for.

While invalidation of the need for grieving may be common with all forms of grief, this is often more prevalent when grieving a pet. As in Lac's poem, sometimes we may have to demand our right to grieve. However, we hope readers of this book will also learn how to better support those who are grieving. They can begin to appreciate the power of sitting with grief. They can begin to appreciate the importance of sitting with those who are grieving without trying to take pain away—to be with them in their grief.

The Decision

The ending of the lives of our pets is frequently a decision we have to make. While many have to make similar decisions with our human loved ones, this decision is the norm with pets. We cannot talk with them about when they believe the suffering is too much; we must make the decision on our own, and this is difficult.

We learn to communicate with our pets in nonverbal ways. Observation becomes a way of showing love. They watch us intensely out of love and learn what we are trying to tell them with our actions, and we do the same with them. In this lifelong relationship of engagement through observation, we are able to listen with our eyes. We listen to our pets by watching and observing the changes, especially in their final days.

In "Dante's Last Days," much of the poem focuses on my (Louis) listening to Dante: hearing the difference in his whine and howl, watching the change in his behaviors, noticing the differences in his gait, understanding his need for proximity and comfort. It is a painful listening. At times, just watching him walk would bring tears to my eyes, though he showed no overt signs of pain. It is listening that most people could not understand because they have not experienced the relationship over time. It is a listening based on that special way of communicating that we developed together through careful observation.

A poem by Patrick Dixon, "Falling," also documents the painful observation of the last days, witnessing the struggle of accepting the meaning of the message. Dixon watched his pet fall and struggle because of his aging body. He listened and he loved, and he tried to make the best decision for his pet.

It is difficult to accept that a beloved pet is dying. How do we know if we are keeping them alive because we do not want to let go? In the poem "Ready," Gamble writes,

> *You'll know when she's ready,*
> the vet said,
> *Look into her eyes, she'll tell you.*
> For the next week I slept on the floor beside her,
> not wanting to see the look that said
> *Let me go.*

It is not as simple as Gamble's vet suggests. We often do not know. And when we do, we question ourselves and often wrestle with our denial of the reality. Even when we know it is the right decision, it is not easy. We don't want to let go. Our time to say goodbye may not align with their time to be ready to let go.

In "For My Jenny," Zelke-Windau documents the last moments of Jenny's life through the burial. As we read the poem, we witness the journey. We see the reaction to the vet's attempt at comfort:

> "She's gone already," he said. "No pain."
> What is no pain? There is pain. I have pain,
> And longing, and memories.

Comfort is difficult at these moments. The feelings are not comfortable, but we seek to become comfortable with the existence of these feelings. When friends try to give comfort, it eludes the recipient. The only comfort that can be offered is the comfort of presence, which does not take the pain away but somehow helps make it a little more tolerable.

Guides and Caretakers

In the poem "Guide Dogs," Greening speaks to the ability of dogs to guide us on our emotional journey. They seem to innately have the wisdom of an experienced therapist who knows how to help find the pain within and then gently say, "It's okay. It doesn't feel good, but this is where we need to be right now."

In the poem, "...of being mothered and mothering," we see how with pets caretaking is a mutual process. We take care of our pets as they take care of us. They become our comforters. We can learn from our pets when we open ourselves to their wisdom. In "Melting Snow," Moats shares two separate stanzas that speak to this learning through the wisdom of our pets:

> Wintery woods,
> The peacefulness of falling snow,
> Your favorite playground.
> A good day to die.
>
> Snow is falling,
> Snow is melting,

An understanding that you already had.
No wonder you allowed it to blanket you.

Helping Those Grieving from Pet Loss

It is not comfortable to be with those who are grieving. As therapists, we have learned the importance and value of pain and grieving. These experiences are not "bad" or pathological experiences, but part of the tapestry of life. When people are deprived of their right to experience their pain and grief, it only makes things worse.

The impulse to pull people from their suffering is natural and makes sense. We want those who we care about to feel better. Yet, the way to do this is not by pulling them from their pain but rather by joining them in their pain. To help those who grieve we must strive to become more comfortable sitting in the midst of the pain with the ones we love. We must strive to be a stable, consistent source of comfort in the midst of the discomfort.

Often, words are not needed and tend to get in the way. Presence—simple presence—is what is needed. If we can be in the room with the grieving person and be present with them, this is all they need. To be present, we must put aside our phones and computers and other things that distract us, and just be there, in the moment. This is a powerful gift, but it is not as easy as it may sound. To just be present with someone who is hurting takes commitment, patience, and the ability to be with one's own pain and discomfort. Henri Nowen (1979) shared the following:

> The friend who can be silent with us in a moment of despair or confusion, who can stay with us in an hour of grief or bereavement, who can tolerate not knowing, not curing, not healing, and face us with the reality of our powerlessness, that is the friend who cares. (as cited in Walsh, 1988, p. 19)

This book is created to be that compassionate friend who shares in the bereaved's pain rather than advise them how to get over, get past, or get through the pain.

The Story of *Our Last Walk*

The editors have long been pet lovers, with dogs being our pet of choice. Over the years we have known each other, we have shared stories of pets, aging pets, and pet loss. And we have shared our poems about pets as well. In 2015, Mike and Louis were presenting on

Capturing Shadows: Poetic Encounters Along the Path of Grief and Loss at the annual Existential-Humanistic Institute Conference. As we discussed the tears shed at Mike's poem, "Melting Snow," we began to formulate the idea for *Our Last Walk*. For each of us, turning to poetry was an automatic response when dealing with the loss of beloved pets.

As we considered our own process of grieving for pets, the idea of the book emerged naturally. There are many levels to this book, which are hinted at in this short introduction. It is a book of friendship. Our relationships with one another provided an important foundation for the book. It is also a book of community. As we began receiving poems, it was easy to begin sensing this community of pet lovers who were coming together to share their love and their loss. It is a story of love—love for our pets. With each tear shed when reading the poems included in this book, one could imagine an even greater love that preceded it. Thus, this is the story of this book: a story of friendship, community, and love.

It is also a book of preparation. As we compiled this book, two of us (Louis and Tom) were facing the impending loss of another beloved pet. Compiling the book became a process of preparing for loss. In the various threads of the story of *Our Last Walk*, we believe something powerful emerged. Our story is one of those threads, but it is joined with many other threads as well.

Using *Our Last Walk* for Grieving and Remembering

We hope that *Our Last Walk* will help readers in a variety of ways on their journey of grieving. For many, reading the poems may be the primary way this book serves their healing. After *Capturing Shadows: Poetic Encounters Along the Path of Grief and Loss* was published, many people shared with us how the book impacted them. A common theme was that the poems helped them feel less alone in their grieving. Others shared that they felt they were given permission to grieve. Some found inspiration through seeing how others faced their grieving. When we offered presentations and workshops based on *Capturing Shadows*, we always included activities encouraging people to write their own poems. Many found healing in writing their own poems after reading or hearing some of the poems in *Capturing Shadows*. As is always true with grieving, there is no one right path.

Writing poetry for healing is different than writing poetry with the intention of creating a work of art. When writing poetry for healing, it is important to let go of the internal critic and not worry about the quality of the poem. While poems written for the purpose of healing often can be good-quality poems, when healing and growth become the primary focus then concern about quality often interferes with the healing process. The focus on quality can even serve to distract one from the powerful emotions driving one to write.

When selecting poems for *Our Last Walk*, we were intentional about including a wide array of poems. As with previous books in this series, we are sure that different readers will be drawn to different poems and authors. The variety of poems allows for readers to find the poems that speak to them. Also, we hope the variety of poems will help people experiment with writing various types of poems and give them the freedom to explore various styles of writing. We chose to focus on poems that are accessible for this volume as well. While more complex poetry can be beautiful and powerful, it can also be intimidating or cause people to focus on rationally trying to understand the poem instead of experiencing it. Therefore, we selected mostly accessible poems that speak directly to the experience of grieving.

Conclusion

The relationships between humans and pets are full of opportunities to experience love, growth, companionship, and pain. Though this book is filled with stories of grief and loss, pain and despair, and unanswered questions and confusion, listen closely to the messages beneath the painful expressions. Listen closely to the valued relationships of love and friendship, relationships worth every ounce of pain endured and enduring.

Our Last Walk will not remove your pain and sorrow, but hopefully will help you to cherish it in a way that offers you freedom to create a productive space for it and to find solace. Our hope is that you will be able to reflect on the pets you have loved, and create a home for those memories, both in spite of your pain and because of your pain.

References

Hoffman, L., & Moats, M. (2015). Introduction: Capturing shadows with poetry. In L. Hoffman & M. Moats (Eds.), *Capturing shadows: Poetic encounters along the path of grief and loss* (pp. 11–26). Colorado Springs, CO: University Professors Press.

Kowalski, G. (2012). *Goodbye, friend: Healing wisdom for anyone who has ever lost a pet* (Rev. ed.). Novato, CA: New World Library.

Walsh, E. (1988). *Grief: How it can help you.* Liguori, MO: Liguori Publications.

Poems

Dante's Last Days

Louis Hoffman

Your whine became different
That's when I first knew
Our way of communicating love
was intent observant
And this day it brought a message
Too painful to hear

Even those last days
In so much pain
You howled at the vet's office
Until everyone greeted you
So much more the extrovert
And you loved indiscriminately

Yet, as they took you to the back
And examined your pain
You wanted out
Your ears lay down
Searching for an exit
Instead of the attention you craved
With all their knowledge and expertise
They could not know the meaning
of this simple behavior
but I knew
and no longer held the tears.

On the way home with bottles
of comfort pills
I cried
You were still here
But what I knew changed everything

That night you cried and cried
'Til it broke my heart
I couldn't take your pain
And just sat with you
Presence seemed to do more

for your pain than the 19 pills
now part of your daily regimen

You now stayed close at my side
Exploring and adventures
No longer a temptation
All you wanted was the comfort
of presence
And I could never give it enough

Those last days
our love grew greater
in the shadow of the end
Now, as I look at the spot on the floor
Where not long ago you lay at my side
I can still feel the warmth
And I feel loved.

Photograph by Louis Hoffman

Stopping

Tom Greening

For years I jogged each morning
to the end of my street and back
accompanied by my dog Demian
until one March morning
he stood still and did not follow me.
I called him. No response.
I ran a few feet, stopped, and called him again.
He turned around and slowly walked back to my house.
That morning marked the end of my youth.
Thirty years later Demian is long dead
and I have stopped jogging.
Now I know how he felt
as he stood there
watching me go on with life
without him.

Melting Snow

Michael Moats

Teardrops melting the freshly fallen snow
A favorite resting place for my old, fat dog.
Heat lamps, doggie doors, and an outside house
All options that you primarily saw as needless.

Demanding, intelligent, and loving.
Your disposition
A familiar one,
Like the other ladies in the home.

First the arthritis,
Then the breathing.
Nothing would stop you
From enjoying the child's play next door.

The barking subsided,
The pace had slowed.
Pleasurable groans
With the rubbing of your ears.

I saw your decline,
I saw your struggle.
Your still strong attitude and wagging tail
Had helped me avoid the decision.

The weather changed
And so did you.
Your stubbornness still present
Beneath the confusion and labored breath.

Wintery woods,
The peacefulness of falling snow,
Your favorite playground.
A good day to die.

I look into your eyes of love
Tired, yet comforted by my broken presence.

280 lbs of weeping flesh
Desire and understanding, in combat.

I share the broth
From my lunch with you.
At first, hesitation, before lapping at our bowl.
Most likely your giving, rather than want.

So tired, you lay.
My breath, too, is labored.
Your head resting against my arm
As I rub your belly with memories of past.

Not ready to make the call
I want to prolong the day.
Loving you too much
To avoid it any longer.

My stomach knotted
Waiting for him to arrive.
Final private moments
Of love and old, puppy kisses.

You continued to speak to me
As you had so many times before.
You became silent and still.
I rubbed you gently long after.

Caressing your ears,
Stroking your fur,
And saying goodbye to a friend,
I walked you as far as I could.

Snow is falling,
Snow is melting,
An understanding that you already had.
No wonder you allowed it to blanket you.

To my old, fat dog
You have given your whole life to me.
Run free, my girl,

Run free!

Teardrops melting the freshly fallen snow...

***

Previously published in *Capturing Shadows: Poetic Encounters Along the Path of Grief and Loss* by Louis Hoffman and Michael Moats. Reprinted with permission.

Photograph by Michael Moats

For My Jenny

Marilyn Zelke-Windau

Oh, my dog girl, I miss you.
The apple tree is shedding white blossom tears.
They fall softly—as soft as your fur—
upon the mound of earth which is now your home.
Wrapped in your pink bicky you came to me
at four weeks old.
Wrapped in your pink bicky you leave me
after fourteen years.

Lie down, my Jenny, and rest now. Rest.
Those back, stiff legs can be still.
It hurt me so to see you fall—
wobbly like a newborn foal—
your look with fear, not knowing
why your body couldn't function.

Those big brown eyes, lately clouded,
reached out to my heart as they always could and told me—
it must be nearly over now.

Help me, hold me, and yet I must try to rise.

Little licks on my bare, hair-matted leg
with your nose pressed to me,
we rode to meet our last farewell.
"It's ok. It's ok, my Jen," I said, knowing it wasn't.
Why do we lie to comfort those we love?

Your last protection—those narrow, hard to find veins—
couldn't win.
"She's gone already," he said. "No pain."
What is no pain? There is pain. I have pain,
and longing, and memories.
No plastic bag, no box. I'll take her.
I spread out the blanket in the trunk, your first tomb.

I must dig. It's something I have to do. In a blur of disbelief.
Keep the dirt off her blanket.
You were so heavy and still as I laid you down.
A little groan came from your mouth and I looked—
hoping beyond hope that you were coming back to me.
But no.

I tried to make you comfortable, placing each foot just so
and putting your ears down.
Oh, how they used to flop when you'd run.
I made sure your bicky covered you
before I gave you your earth blanket,
telling you I loved you with each rush of dirt.

You weren't at the bottom of the stairs this morning,
clicking your nails on the hardwood floor.
No more signals to me upstairs that you were waiting for me.
I held your food dish and cried.
Your brush is in the basement. Your hair is on the car seat.
Your corner is empty.
I'm empty.
You won't curl up at my feet for comfort anymore,
warming me with gentle love.
The love is still here, the warmth—
only to be shared now in thought and memory.
My cub dog.

Cece

Joy Hoffman

The violence around your departure
And our complacency,
As you wandered out the patio door
Out of sight
Out of mind
Believing you would stay nearby
Even in old age, poor eyesight and hearing

The moment you entered that backyard
Curious
Exploring
You did not hear the Shepherd behind you

We had hope
And yet we knew
Shaking
Scared
Broken
We knew
And just like that you were gone

But not out of sight
Or out of mind
Still nearby
I see you
I hear you
And I wish we could start that day over again
Every damn day, I wish we could start over.

This photo was taken on Cece's last walk.
Photograph by John Hoffman

Her Fella

Carl "Papa" Palmer

she rubs my head
runs her fingers across my face
and she cries
she holds me tight
her head next to mine
and she cries
I tell her that nothing has changed
I try to explain
but she doesn't understand
she hasn't understood anything I've said
for the past five years

we've been together since she was a little girl
we understood each other then
she'd talk with me for hours
she'd look into my eyes
tell me all her secrets
evenings on the porch swing
or in the yard, laughing and playing
or in her room, lying on her bed
watching her every move

I learned so much from her
she taught me what she liked, what she didn't like
she'd ruffle my hair. Give me a hug and a kiss
speak to me in her special way
she called me her Fella
she'd say, "Come here, Fella"
and I'd be right there by her side
ready for anything she wanted to do
that was then

as she grew older, became a teenager
became busy, became popular
she had less time for our long walks together
our talks were what I missed the most
I was still her Fella, still there for her

but she was outgrowing me
soon she didn't talk with me at all
sometimes at me but never a conversation
and sometime during that time
she stopped hearing my words altogether

now barely out of her teenage years
time seems to have gone by so quickly
our fifteen years together
her, so full of life
so vibrant, so youthful
but me, I feel so old
as if I have aged seven years
for each one of hers
some days I feel at least a hundred years old

and now she treats me like that too
lately she's spending more time with me
I love that she's doing that
it's just the crying
I wish she wasn't so sad
she holds me close
rocks me and she cries
she carries me everywhere
won't let me do a thing
does everything for me
and she cries

we get into her car, I love to watch her drive
she used to look my way and smile
today she stops several times
takes me in her arms
and cries   and cries   and cries

we enter the cold, bright room, yet I feel peace
I feel her tremble
as the doctor shaves my wrist
just above my paw
the needle is withdrawn
I feel warmth and happiness

we romp and play in the yard
her and I
laughing and shouting
in words we both understand
just like before
before she began to cry

A Soft, Yellow Prayer

Diana Norma Szokolyai

for Napra Forgo, the sweet, yellow parrotlet

Her still, warm, little body in my left palm,
I want to bathe her,
and see her sweet and lively again,
as lemon peel spritzes its sugary tang onto the fingers.

It is sudden, from a bird to
a soft, yellow prayer in my hand.
Transformation happens
at the speed the sun turns the sky pink early in the morning.

I imagine a bird's breath,
like a woodwind player
breathes in
between measures of Bach's *Partita in A minor.*

My bird's tiny lungs and air sacs
no longer expand and contract.
They are thin as Thai paper lanterns,
laid down with their lost light.

At the Baghdad Pet Market

Tom Greening

Creation is designed so that "...a large proportion of all animals should pass their existence in tormenting and devouring other animals."
J.S. Mill, 1874

At the Baghdad pet market
after not one but two explosions
the specially trained pigeons flew away,
and the boys' hopes for money
flew also, and their blood ran,
and the bodies of people and dogs
and monkeys and sheep
lay on top of each other.
"Red in tooth and claw" cried Tennyson,
and with that in mind
the bombers had packed their bombs
with ball bearings.
Two hours after the explosions
some boys were back
and, like their goats,
were stubbornly hopeful
that it is possible to live
even in such a world.

Drool

Kylee Cushman

Old dog...
Your body too big to carry
up the hill to the grave and the wheelbarrow
we used so undignified as your head
kept rolling over the side
with every dip and stone
in the field.

Straining and struggling we lowered
your body down into the hole
onto your favorite plaid bed
a crisp white sheet to cover
then heavy, wet
shovels of soil.

Damp earth
filled my nostrils until
I could barely draw
my next breath.

It's been three months since that syringe
of blue liquid spread throughout
your veins and your fast rasping
breath brought permanent end
to days of pain.

I stored my heartache in the basement with
your bowls, your leash, and wiped
your nose prints from the front windows where
you patiently watched for our return.

Today, under the dining room table
where you lay at meal time
feigning disinterested sleep yet
salivating, waiting for a juicy
scrap of chicken skin,
a slice of sharp cheddar,

flaky salmon licked
from fingers

is a dried puddle
of dog drool and I just
can't bring myself to
mop it up now that snow has covered
your white spirit and snow has buried
the granite post upon
which we hung the red
nylon collar.

Your tags which jingled
always now no longer
visible.

He Got Loose

Richard Bargdill

On the day that I die
I hope I
run loose
On the day that I die
I hope I
run loose
People forget that freedom
is something
you choose
Some day
I hope I
can be like you.

They train us
with whips and leashes
and the hangman's noose
If you play, laugh, or smile
they'll treat you
like a fool
My inner child
got chained up
while I attended school
On the day that I die
I hope I
run loose.

They teach us to *Sit Down*
Shut Up and *Don't*
Make a Move
You have to *LISTEN*
to your masters
Obey every rule
But if they leave
the door open
no one can fault you

On the day
that you died
you ran loose.

Love's Labor's Lost or Why I Don't Own Pets

Carolyn Martin

Three chameleons
disappeared
into our bamboo shades.
The horny lizard's
soft-curled back
amazed
then,
like goldfish
in their hazy bowl,
flipped
its down-side up.
Unamused,
dad booted out
the lab who
slurped
his cabbage soup.
The speckled mutt
arrived
one day,
ran
away the next.
Need more
reasoning?
A droop-face cop
charged
our summer yard
and shot
two frothing pups.
My heart
can't bear
another crack.
I fall in love
too hard,
too fast.

Making Iced Tea

Kim M. Baker

She had long ago decided that life was possible, if not actually gratifying, if one reduced the risk.
"Falling Slowly," Anita Brookner

1.

I refuse to have any more animals, he said.
I can't take the pain of letting go.

2.

Gratifying, a word like making iced tea,
enjoyable, two lumps please,
with tiny blocks of ice that
make drinking nice on a cloudless day
when I should be doing the laundry
or cutting the lawn.

3.

I can still picture her, there,
compacting the path around the fence line,
fur white like bearing witness to risk.
She will surely report back
in ruffs and woofs,
the presence of roustabout cats
and suspect spaniels.
Her coat feels for the slightest breeze
that might relieve our August oppression.
I begin to brush her gallant fur,
whisper *good girl* into alert ears,
But she yowls, *Not now.*
There is someone at the gate.

4.

There is nothing now but grieving
and making iced tea.
Weak as my release.
Unsweetened as this freedom.
A sprig of mint.
But there is nothing fresh here.
The fence line is not secure anymore.
Someone opened the gate
and death sauntered right in
disguised as a summer breeze.

5.

I scan the yard and think
about the pain of letting go.
And the velvet ears,
the years of canine antics,
the endearing, unconditional love.

6.

As I make iced tea
brewed strong and sweet,
I watch a new her, there,
securing the fence line,
fur black like laughing at fear.

***

An abridged version of this poem was previously published on
http://www.origamipoems.com. Reprinted with permission.

Prints

Susan Claire Glass

Morning, and the window where He guarded
our waking is empty.
The young dog, belly up, laughs raucously,
Bangs the day with her tail
orders all yawns to the kitchen.

Old Dog, always patient,
reverently nosed in beside her just about now
laid his wise life muzzle print on my left arm
And so blessed, we all adjourned.

I open the side door so that Young Dog may set the mischievous
garden in order.
What choice have I?
Young Dog was born with springs attached and no brakes.
She's down the cement step before He, within his body's mutiny,
can even find the threshold.
Those last days, we balanced him on our hands
Let him flop front half first, down the incline to safety.
We prayed for gravity to be kind.

Night-time, I trek from den, to garden, to sleep again.
His wise ghost tracks me
through the between-room silences where claws hesitantly tap
wood.
I reach out, touch feather air, phantom muzzle; only a furnace draft.
"It's ok," I tell his soul. Yet I find
I'm still at fault
as though it's my grief that's holding him here
because finally, grief is all I have left.

Today brings a rain reprieve, and green tips the apricot branches.
There are sun dapples in the strawberry bed where Old Dog took his
summer naps.
I touch the leaves, surprised by their give, and the imprint they
remember.

Scrappy Boy

J. Blair Cano

Unexpectedly you entered my life
A young and scrappy young pup, who nobody wanted
At the same time, I was a young and scrappy young woman
Who thought she needed no one
With each other we grew
You became my fierce protector and I your constant love
Together we matured
We both became predictable and dependable
Together we started a family
You not only protected me, but also my children
I always felt safe with you near
When I cried, you licked my tears
When my babies cried, you licked their tears
As if to convey that with you near, all would be ok
When you fell ill, I held you
When you couldn't walk, I carried you
As you left this earth, I cried profusely and uncontrollably
In a way I have not ever cried for a human loss
I still do today, two years after you have left me
Losing you in my life has left a desperate void
I swell with tears just thinking of you
Missing you and your companionship
Missing your love and kisses
Reflecting back on all the years we shared together
The moments and milestones we shared can never be
recreated
They are of memories past; I reflect on them and you with
warm
fondness
I still love you so much, my sweet baby Scrappy Boy

What Can I Say?

Robert Carroll

We finished moving all the furniture,
switched our bedroom with my office,
so now I'm writing in a room with an eastern exposure,
the sun streaming through the moats in the blinds.
The trees are different on this side.
Some loom over me to my left,
others step up the hill to the gardens above,
and if I stand up and look to my right,
there's a crack of ocean sparkling in the sunlight.

The gardeners' lawn mowers crack the quiet with their sputter
and the blues of the sky soften into mist over the water
and the sounds from the parking lot are of a world waking up.
This will be a good place to write.

The bedroom's better too, more ventilation at night.
The ocean breezes make the breathing easier,
and the sounds of the traffic from Sunset are only a muffled hum,
something to sleep to when my mind wanders to oblivion,
and the dreams come.

My golden retriever, Ben, walked down a boat ramp into the water.
He walked out and down until he was completely covered over.
I could see his sweet face look up to me
the surface of the water flat as glass.
He had a mournful look of love
as if he wanted me to know he was all right
but alone, separated from me above.

And I knew Ben's sweet face told me something
of my own, closed under by life's pressure
but wanting to burst up in the fragrant air
the sweet smells of summer
springtime in winter
the smell of wet hair
tumbling tumbling tumbling in space
where up is not up, where there is

no there, and the timeless presence of my dog remembered
tells me I still have much to learn from history
because Ben is still with me, even though he's only in memory
but the history of his life had a presence in my own
from the time he was a puppy and I slept with him
to calm his whimpering, to the time he grew into doggy adolescence
and got strong like my son.
And then he came into his prime with his flaming golden hair
as I stepped into mine with my coppery beard
but then he turned gray, as of course we all must—
father to son, rust to rust—
and I felt my decline measured in the life of my dog
as his hips went limp, my father's legs gave out
and his kidneys stopped, and his heart clogged
and his skin developed hemorrhages that pulled him down
and Ben, my beauty, condensed all of our three generations
into his fourteen short years of life
then he visited me in my dream
his golden fur glistening in the sunlight.

He walked straight into the water
and when he was below
he looked at me and waited
as he's waiting for me now
to rise and break the surface
or to dive and meet his presence
the spirit is among us
the seaweed in browns and golds floats
to the surface and sways in the current.
I am strong. I am free. I am here at my desk

and the Spanish-speaking gardeners turn off their lawn mowers
and sit down to rest, and it's summer and it's sparkling
and the breeze sways the branches
and my bedroom is my office
as I sit at my desk
and gaze out the widow
and feel grateful for all I have left.

***

"What Can I Say?" was previous published in *Amazing Change: Poetry of Healing and Transformation* by Robert Carroll. Published by Bombshelter Press, 2009. Reprinted with permission.

Guide Dogs

Tom Greening

We each have a well of sadness in us,
often buried.
Dogs know how to find it
and take us there
by their dying.
They are all guide dogs
for the journey we resist taking,
and they give their lives to us
so we may live deeper.

Into the Motion of Other Things

Enid Shomer

There's a lamp clamped to my desk and on its blue
enamel shade the overhead fan, reflected
as a tiny pinwheel, spins as if to show
how the atoms inside must move—electrons
orbiting, smaller agitated particles
slamming and humming within the thick
metal cone, like the traffic of blood cells
just beneath the skin. Outside, leaves quake
on stilled twigs, soil heaves up, grain
by grain. Grit floats on the tide of my eye,
today's excuse to grieve for you, gone now,
not into stillness, but into the motion
of other things, like the water that spilled
as the child carried it to you in her hands.

***

"Into the Motion of Other Things" was previous published in *This Close to Earth* by Enid Shomer. Published by University of Arkansas Press, 1992.

Not the Last Goodbye

Dori Appel

for Shadow

Your shorn coat lies on
the stainless steel table
like a flattened ghost of you,
tattered scraps waiting
to be swept into the trash,
while I bring you home
naked and demented,
your blind eye sucking itself
further back into your head,
as though trying to catch
a glimpse of who you were.

All day you hunch your
trembling body against
a kitchen cabinet,
your mind emptied of
memory and response.
I say your name,
softly at first, then louder
when you don't come to me
or even turn your head,
and finally I understand
that you don't know who I am,
or why I'm calling
"Shadow! Shadow! Shadow!"
from some far place.

Sonnet to a Dead Cat

Juleigh Howard-Hobson

"There are no ordinary cats."
— Colette

Her body is nothing, really, a heap
Of rumpled fur, clipped nails, long whiskers that
Have ceased to twitch, a tail that no longer
Hangs just so, waiting to counterweight leaps
To couches from windowsills, ears gone flat,
Eyes shut, mouth closed. Memory is stronger.

A cat owns its people, never forget.
I bought the food, the toys, paid for the vet.

That cat lived with me for 12 years or so
Meowing for more cat food, shedding hair,
Chewing on corners of books. She would go
Out then in, then out again, then in, stare
At me unyieldingly if I was slow
To open doors. She's gone. I don't know where.

Requiem for Golden Things

Mary Davies Cole

for China and Wookie

Late one November day, we lost her.
For several nights she had huddled
close to my body, but the morning
of the day she died,
she crept far, far into the woods
resting there, gazing back at the house,
her golden coat in the orange leaves.
The seizure came in the afternoon.
Her name was China. She was cremated.
We kept her ashes in a little wooden box.

When we moved the next spring
far away to a salt marsh-lined road,
we buried her in the garden,
under the root-ball of a young Chinese
Dogwood tree. Every year
when it burst into bloom, I imagined
her ashes feeding each new pink-ridged blossom,
her spirit running free
in the sap of the supple branches.

I still follow the road around the marsh
in the slant light of late afternoon.
There is another dog now, who has also grown old.
We watch the wetlands breathe
with the rise and fall of the tides.
The light changes hourly. It is fall again,
so the songbirds are leaving. The egrets will go soon,
and the Great Blue Heron has flown
from the tidal flats to an inner pond.
Salt-marsh hay has turned a soft golden hue.
We used to gather it for mulch.

Before long, we will be leaving the marsh.
Leaving the weeping birch and cherry trees,
the elegance of the Japanese maple.

On the path behind our house
a new two-inch hole leads to a burrow.
A family of voles is moving in,
or rabbits, or ground squirrels. Who knows?
... The red-tailed hawk knows, precisely,
and the screech owls in the old gnarled oak.

I have learned to breathe in and out,
with this watery changeable land.
I have learned that things are never the same
even two hours later.
I have known the wisdom of good dogs,
and we've learned to walk quietly
near the nesting birds, so to hear their songs
rise out of salt grass and common reed.
When the winter winds sweep across silver ice floes,
and seagulls and crows make arcs through the frigid blue air,
we won't be here to watch them sail in that sparkling world.
We are only here together, for this brief moment's gaze,
in the span of a too-short life.

"Wookie" Photograph by Mary Davies Cole.

Don't Forget

Robin Winter

Don't forget your way home
however deep the night and the bewilderment of stars.
Use their light to find your way, swift
pad through stems of grass, and tumbled rock. Any
way, long or short; but come.
You can hear us listening in the black,
halting our breath, hoping we hear
a whisper between branch stir,
and dew sounding in leaves
like small feet.

I feel we will be waiting forever; this night,
all nights,
little cat.

After Sixteen Years

Steven K. Smith

I picked up the old 4-10 shotgun
my dad had left me and a shovel,
and led my dog into the field.
He could hardly walk.
Arthritis crippled his hips,
throat nearly closed by cancer,
but his tail wagged his happiness
as he struggled out after me,
no doubt remembering quail
flushed from the tall grass
or rabbits chased but not caught
just for the exercise of his hunter's instinct.

By the giant oak tree at the edge of the forest
I stopped — waited for him to catch up.
A few purple-brown leaves still hung
on the spreading branches
already shed of their acorns,
where we'd stopped to rest many times before.
Where I'd never be able to rest again.

"Sit" I commanded.
Like the veteran bird dog he was,
he obeyed at once, and I patted his head.
"Good boy," I said, in a voice made of dry leaves.
I stepped back, raised the gun and aimed,
saw him cock his head, confused,
as I looked through the sights.
"This is different," he seemed to say.

Half blinded by tears
I dug his grave.
I should have dug it first,
but then my courage would have failed me.

***

"After Sixteen Years" was previously published in *Whatever House We Come From* by Jennifer Bosveld (Editor) Pudding House Publications, Columbus, OH, 2006; also published in *After Enough Time* by Steven K. Smith, Pudding House Chapbook series, Columbus, OH, 2011. Reprinted with permission.

Mortal Dogs

Tom Greening

Ralph’s predecessors had died off.
Years ago I had lain on the kitchen floor with Damian
explaining, asking permission,
to put him to sleep.
Anthropomorphism is often a refuge of sentimentalists,
but he seemed to understand
even if I didn't.
His successor, Mop, a fluffy cockapoo,
became daffy and incontinent,
but it still took my wife months to convince me
that her "quality of life" was nil,
as ours was becoming.
Next, Mop’s daughter, Runt, declined unexpectedly,
The vet wanted $900 just to prop her up,
and could not promise immortality.
So then we were down to one dog,
Ernie, a dachshund left behind by our daughter
when she left us behind.
I called him "the rotund rodent"
and he endured such insults,
believing he was the survivor
who was going to outlive me,
but he didn’t.
And then I adopted his successor,
Ralph, also a dachshund, from a rescue shelter,
also, like me, irritable and mortal.
I did him no favor by keeping him alive
after his mind went
and he staggered around the house
like I now sometimes do.

... of being mothered and of mothering

Betz King

Mom broke most of my bones
when I was 9 weeks old.
The end of having a mom.

Grandma dropped dead as we fought over
whether I could watch the fireworks with a boy.
Also the end of having a mom.

"Family" let me live with strangers
rather than make room for me.
More mothers, more endings.

Strangers found me worthy for a time,
But... eventually evicted me as unworthy.
The ultimate ending of anything resembling mothering.

Of course I married the wrong guy.
He left with my fertility.
The end of being a mom.

Then the Paisley-puppy arrived, with superpowers of radical
empathy and loving kindness. Opener of the ways, she leapt over my
heart-barricades in a single bound.
An invitation into the mysteries of mothering.

I learned her noises, her breaths, her eyebrow positions
and tail communications.
I woke in the night for no reason to find her needing me.
The beginning of being a mom.

She wore her love for me like a shawl of the softest yarn.
She could envelope the whole therapy room in that cape.
The beginning of being mothered.

For a decade of days, her eyes lit when I entered a room,
while she brought the same to my clients.
The full-blown experience of having a mom.

Staying longer than any other, she decreed me ever-worthy.
Wedding ring bearer, dissertation coach,
intuitive empathic best friend.
The experience of a mother and a daughter... a daughter and mother.

I midwifed her cancer-ridden transition into sacred space.
By far the hardest call to service in my life.
The end of having a mom...
The end of being a mom....
...of being mothered and of mothering.

But at least she taught me, and at least I learned
(better late than never),
about the heartbreaking joys and sorrows found
within the mysteries of being mothered, and of mothering.

Photograph courtesy of
Michigan School of Professional Psychology

You Are Not Here

Ken Wolman

Pushkin, d. September 9, 2006

While you were dying I stroked your coat.
It was not beautiful, it never was,
but I stroked your coat because it was yours
as years before I healed my unmarried self
by stroking that same coat,
crying as I cried this morning,
by loving you not because you were
the most beautiful cat I ever saw but because
you loved me and wanted me now not to hold you close
as I'd held you close, but to let you go
to Outside Over There, but you were not there
and now you are here.

All Things Blanche:
24 Years of Infinity

Rozann Kraus

with no reference to that southern belle,
your pristine luminosity, candid camouflage
shimmering kitten destined to be
Blanche
our first pet.

early years of stealth pursuits
barely known to exist
you were the opposite of
a lap cat
consenting to sunfilled photo ops
aloof window percher

as any godless ruler
your rare purr kept us
mildly infatuated with hope
that you'd deign to be demonstrative;
not just when we fed you

Taekout too large and frowzy
Buddha bridged the gap
this hat trick of beasts
colluding forbidden larceny;
you were the only one allowed upstairs

in piled years, we stroked your strokes
as each new life released a sweetened you
a kitness purr and hunt for love
your presence became insistent
as your need for community
grew as noisily as your hunger
then clockwise was your ballast
circling for sustenance
endless laps around the island.
your people left and returned
you grew a homecoming meander

joining us on the floor, at the table
on the couch
in our bed, on our heads
and in our hearts.

Pieces of challah for a Shabbat kiss
peanut butter and dispossessed plates
tormenting Rae with your whiteness
somewhere you stopped jumping on the counters
relocating your pee to cast your vote
countless rehearsals of abstinence and denial
you always were you the next day.
marker of eternity, you let us know
this time you said goodbye.

Alone in Grief

Betsy Snider

I. October

October is a strange month.
Dogs die and a mind goes astray,
gets lost in the ganglia of the amygdala.

Perhaps dogs, like the mind, can no longer
endure another season of deep freeze,
that lonely cold when wind is the only companion,
when despair falls like snow over the soul.

By spring, the dogs are buried
and the mind, which was lost, has been found.

II. Solo Fall

I walk around the lake
with no dogs to accompany me,
only red and yellow leaves
that blow across dirt roads.
I catch the sun as it angles
further south casting diamonds
across deep blue water
ruffled by the wind.

I am alone in a vast wilderness
of dying trees; water thickening
with the cold; brown ferns
curled over thatched grass;
and everywhere silence drops
as heavy as dew at dawn.

III. Winter Echoes

The sun slants low
behind the mountain.
I walk on the narrow road

amidst cabins closed and shuttered
for the winter. I hear a dog bark
from inside a cottage guarded
by unbroken drifts across the door.

I stop, startled. As silence seeps
into my bones, I hear the dog
bark again, inside the abandoned
chamber of my heart.

Surrender

Andrew Shattuck McBride

Bigglesworth remains alert, loving, attentive.
He's very ill and in some pain. I'm in denial.

His decline seems sudden: he can't leap three feet
to kitchen tabletop to check up on me, to sprawl

over a piece of writing I'm working on. I pick
Bigglesworth up and place him on the table

in front of me. Through tears I read a poem
I wrote for him in late 2012—so recently—

"Bigglesworth and I Bat the Puck *Hope*
and Seek Sustenance." He listens but is listless.

There's little to hope for; the veterinarian—
kind, humane, full of empathy—advises me

that it's time to say good-bye to Bigglesworth.
There's little sustenance: he drinks some water,

isn't interested in dry food or canned food,
cat treats or catnip, or a crumb of cheddar

cheese I try tempting him with. For days
he seems unable to sleep, his meows closer

and closer to plaintive cries. His weight loss
so gradual, he still seems sleek under super-fine,

soft long brown-black hair. My denial gives way
to surrender (*surrender*, as how Bigglesworth

lay draped over my left shoulder countless times,
allowing me to pet him without complaint).

My world contracts to Bigglesworth

and our final night together

after thirteen-and-a-half years.
Even with the bedroom door open,

Hobie Cat and Angel sleep elsewhere.
They know. I lie in bed reading. Biggleswort h

rests next to me, our bodies touching, his side
to my knee. His head is up, his front paws

tucked in under his chest,
tail out from his body.

To the end he remains alert,
loving, attentive.

I tell him, *I'm sorry. Please forgive me.*
In the veterinary clinic I surrender,

look in Biggleswort h's eyes, tell him
No more pain. I love you.

I close his eyes, weep unashamedly.
Good-bye, sweet prince.

Caesar at 14 Years

Amy Miller

Through the dark glass
of the back door,
I can't see
if the cat's still there.

Outside, the quiet tick
of rain. Lately he's taken
to a grove
of thick bamboo,
the tumor grown too wide
for him to lie
on bare earth, hard stone.

With the night's breath,
the curtain
waves open,
waves closed.

I see him now
under the patio's shelter,
his sharp spine
a soft orange brush,
his ears tracking
every small sound.

Photograph by Amy Miller

Memento Mori – Annie

Betsy Snider

I. Annie As She Ages

I look into her eyes,
muddy pools
faded with age.
I whisper her name.
She moves her head,
ears perked.
Her tail wags
and she is
the puppy I found
thirteen years ago,
playing tag with cars
on a busy street
by a city park,
alone.

Now,
her grizzled muzzle
grins back at me.
She pants, breath
a pungent mix
of dog food
and grass,
licks my face
as I murmur
into ears
that twitch
as I speak
her name,
again.

II. The Call

I phone the doctor to set up a time
when he can make a house call.
You'd think, after so many times,

it would get easier, the pain
would dull, the tears dry up.

But I find myself unable to talk
without a tell-tale quiver,
a thickening of my voice
so that I must cough before
I wail and moan my misery.

I look over at Annie
who stretches out on the floor,
eyes rimmed in gray, grizzled
muzzle, puzzled by my voice,
the tears streaming down.

She gets up, totters a few steps,
then collapses as her legs give way,
her knees no longer able to bear
her slight frame, frail and wasted,
as her tail curls under her body.

It is time, I tell the vet. After 14 years,
I must say good bye to my constant
companion who will join the others
in the Elysian fields of my dreams.

We calmly discuss
days and times.
I hang up
and howl.

III. Evening Ramble

I walk up the rutted road.
There - in the corner of my eye
she stands, almost hidden
by dusk as it spreads
over bare trees and tall pines.
I stare straight ahead
where Annie trots, turns back
as if to ask, "Where are you?"

I know if I look sideways,
I will see only trees, sentinels
to guard me from the ghosts that gather
in the corners of my heart.

IV. Annie in the Shadows

She sits on the side of the road
and waits for me, her tail a metronome
that keeps time with the beat of her heart,
her muzzle midnight black again,
while I drive through endless hours
down dusty roads and across
a landscape littered with bones.

I know she is there and I am coming
home at the end of the day, at last.

V. Annie

A stray, she wandered into my life
found an empty space and curled up.
She's dead now. My empty spaces
are filled with ghosts.

I Didn't Want to Write Today

Robert Carroll

I didn't want to write today.
I didn't want to write
I took Ben to the vet today,
lifted him into the back seat
and laid him down.

I didn't want to write
the man in the blue scrub suit
put Ben on the gurney and
wheeled him in through the back door
not the front
where all the others held their dogs
on laps and on chains.

I didn't want to write
the little green room on the left was
where we spent our last few minutes together
or that the doctor told us it was time.

I didn't want to write
it was easy to find the vein
and the liquid was blue
and when the doctor aspirated Ben's blood
into the icy blue anesthetic
death became purple
and in ten seconds he was gone
just a breath long and deep,
and then gone.
And I didn't want to write
Susan thought it was peaceful
as I watched his eyes sink.

And when his breathing stopped
the air left me too
and my tears stung
and that's when
I thought of my father

whose road's the same
whose path's the same
down and up and down.

And when we took the long ride home
we could still smell Ben in the back.
His fur blanketed the back seat.
And when we got home
in the late afternoon
and I opened the door
as I always do
and I checked for messages
but there weren't any
I told Susan
I'd meet her upstairs
then I went to the garage
and got his dish
because it was late
and time to eat
and I forgot he was dead.
Already, I forgot.

And I thought, who can I call now?
And again I thought of my father.
Then I heard his voice,

It will be all right boy.
I know it hurts,
but it will be all right.

***

"I Didn't Want to Write Today" was previous published in *Amazing Change: Poetry of Healing and Transformation* by Robert Carroll. Published by Bombshelter Press, 2009. Reprinted with permission.

Thomas

Sherri Wright

I didn't want to see
bony back, blank stare,
back legs failing,
high numbers on the renal tests.

I didn't want to hear
it's not a curable disease,
he's over fifteen,
he's had a good life,

away from the hoarder,
the man with a broom,
the shelter, his aching howl
in the night.

After cancer,
diabetes, injections under the skin,
four trips to Florida,
I thought he'd live forever.

I didn't want to see, so I scrubbed
pee stains and vomit,
cleaned up litter five times a day,
brushed his hair, sewed him a fleece blanket,

bought him soft velvet steps to climb onto the bed,
pushed pills down his throat,
fed him tuna at 3 am, salmon at 4,
stroked his back until,
he purred himself to sleep.

Now I see.

The empty bed, the folded blanket,
his hair on my sleeves.

Teacher

Laura A. Gundy

You taught me how to be a friend
To be silly without critique
To sit without words
To truly forgive and forget
To accept
You taught me how to love myself
Without condition
Without judgment
Without the distorted image of society
You taught me how to appreciate the world
To find peace on a long walk
To embrace all my senses
To know the true joy of a lazy summer day soaking up the afternoon sun
You taught me how to be a parent
To reprioritize
To learn responsibility
To nurture, care for, and love
And through it all you taught me unconditional love
To find my happiness through yours
To find personal joy through the joy of another
And in the end to make the hardest decision of my life...
To walk through my own pain by releasing you from yours
You were more than my pet. You were my teacher. My friend
You loved unconditionally
You expected nothing in return
You loved me for me
Dear Friend I miss you
I love you
I thank you

Let Me Grieve

Veronica Lac

Sadness seeps through the cracks of the dam I built
It buckles under the strain
Warning of the floods that are yet to come
Beware the waves
Shoring up all the strength I can muster
against the deluge ahead
Knowing that the dam will break
I'm fighting in vain

Relief as the floods crash through
I feel the reprieve.
No longer the need to hold the dam, I now release
Pretense is pointless, grief has struck
the waves are tumbling
I drown in the flood
Gasping for air that fails to revive
There's sweet surrender in not living the lie

Don't tell me to be strong
or say I'll be okay.
I know this to be true
and still I hate goodbyes.
In time, I know, I will return
in a different form and my heart intact
once more pieced together,
once more I'll thrive
But for now, let me grieve
in order that I may survive.

Photograph by Kien Quan Lac

Delilah, When You Died

Ann Cefola

Like Orpheus, I put down my lyre.
I didn't need the underground to open;
I wandered our house room to room.

When divine mercy let me feel you
nestled against me, or rippling outside the bath,
flash at the stair top, I forced myself not

to cry so much. But last night, reaching for what
curled in the wing chair, my hand
plummeted—shamed by vacant air.

Old Dachshund

Tom Greening

You know a dog is getting old and desperate
when he starts making up outlandish lies
that even he knows
you won't believe,
like the one my dachshund told me this morning
about how not one but two big coyotes
came in though the small dog door
and peed in my kitchen.
I just looked at him
and he knew his story wasn't working,
but dachshunds are stubborn
and he stuck to it.
So I got the mop and cleaned up
and scowled at him,
and he defiantly scowled back.

My Cat's Death Poem 9

Joan Wiese Johannes

This time I will not hear her last breath

Her tenacity will not become a metaphor
I will not quote Donne

The recluse cat that shares our home
will not meow from room to room

I will not use the word "keening"
to describe that sound

This time I will wrap her in a towel
and slide her into a pillowcase

The ground will have thawed
I will bury her under the spruce tree

Skunks will not root for bulbs
on her grave

Six red tulips and a daffodil will bloom

***

To Duke

Catherine A. MacKenzie

I caress your silent form
while tears run down
my cheeks, still warm
you are, your fur brown

and white, soft and still.
I don't want you to go.
I feel around me a chill
highlighted by a glow

in memory of years
you existed in my life.
I'll never stop tears
I'll shed with strife,

tears that'll linger on
as I live and breathe
while you are gone.
Inside I may seethe

at death causing pain
and stealing the living,
but though I see no gain
I question my misgiving.

Before I say goodbye
I'll touch you one last time,
I know you'll hear my sigh
when the angels chime.

Faithful pal, go run now,
play with those angels free.
Give me one last meow,
I'll hold you while you flee.

Photograph by Catherine A. MacKenzie

A Good Run

Emily Lasinsky

I always wanted a lab.
A lab-mix was one of my choices,
but your big, brown eyes
connected with my ten-year-old heart.

You had to stay in the basement and outside
due to Mom's allergies,
but that didn't stop me from sneaking you inside to cuddle on the couch.

As my dog, you put up with
uneven haircuts,
nicknames such as Puppernickel, Pupsicle, and Pupperella,
new collars that didn't fit right for the first month,
and baths (I'm sure you would want baths to be emphasized).

As your human, I got a chuckle from
your face when I gave you a haircut,
giving you nicknames,
paw prints on my jeans before going on my first date,
and thinking about what you would say if you could talk.

As I moved into my late teen years,
you seemed more like a chore,
I complained about the tasks that needed to be done to take care of you.
You were *my* dog,
It was *my* job,
Now I wish I had those duties.

Your pace started to slow
and I tried to ignore the obvious decline.
I think you were in denial as well,
continuing to splash through the creek, keeping within ten feet of me on the trail.

Then there was the day I had to carry you outside—

reality set in.
I called your name in a high-pitched voice,
trying to get you pepped up for a walk,
but your legs wouldn't move.
Your eyes told me that you weren't the same dog you used to be.

I cradled your body and carried you up the steps, taking notice of
your weight loss.
I placed you gently on the grass and
it didn't take long for you to start running and sniffing.
You looked back at me as if to say, "I'm okay, Em!"
A brief wave of relief swept through my body...
I knew you were *not* okay.

A week later I took you to the vet and found out that you had
cancer
spreading throughout your body.
Surgery was an option, but it was risky and there was no guarantee
that all of the cancer could be
removed.
I could have chosen to run the risk of you dying on the table,
but I chose to wait it out.
I figured this option would give us more time.

The following two weeks I tried to avoid you,
I didn't want to come to terms with the fact that you didn't have
much time.
It was easier for me to think of you as already gone than see those
big, brown eyes in pain.
The day before you left, I broke down and sobbed over your shaking
body.
After half an hour, my emotional state shifted to one of inner peace.
Your eyes told me that you were ready to go.

You accompanied me for more than half of my life,
I didn't want to see you go,
but I think you'd agree that you had a good run.
Thank you, friend, for enriching my life,
Thank you for the companionship and fun.

Photograph by Emily Lasinsky

Grief

Tom Greening

There is a grief loose in my house,
stalking me, even during the day.
Right now it is under the bed.
I can hear its low growl and feel its menace.
Bright lights and upbeat music don't scare it off.
I don't want to get bitten
and have its toxin get into my bloodstream.
Are there pest control men
who will come to my house and smoke it out?
I should have sealed up the openings
in the foundation, and not left food out
in the kitchen. I resent nature
that evolves such a species.
I'll go to the dog pound and get
a big mean hungry dog
and sic it on the grief.
Let the two of them fight it out,
and both leave me alone.

Where is Your Frizzle-Bee?

Daniel Ari

Bella, obsessed as only
a terrier can be, fetched
and returned her frizzle-bee
until I actually left
the park, even as she stood

panting, waiting for the next
throw. I could fake her out once
before her lucid eyes clenched
on the toy, and further feints
just made her stare and whinny.

When she bumps the wall, I wince,
pained at having left a chair
across her ingrained movements
from her bunk to the back door.
I have to be a better

seeing-eye human to her.
Old lady, come and sit here.

Retriever

Barbara Crooker

If "Heaven is a lovely lake of beer," as St. Bridget wrote,
then dog heaven must be this tub of kibble, where you can push
your muzzle all day long without getting bloat or bellyache.
Where every toilet seat is raised, at the right level
for slurping, and fire hydrants and saplings tell you, "Here.
Relieve yourself on us." And the sun and moon
fall at your feet, celestial frisbees flinging themselves
in shining arcs for your soft mouth to retrieve. Rumi says,
"Personality is a small dog trying to get the soul to play,"
but you are a big dog, with an even larger heart, and you
have redeemed our better selves. Forgive us for the times
we walked away, wanting to do taxes or wash dishes
instead of playing fetch or tugger. In the green field
of heaven, there are no collars, no leashes, no delivery trucks
with bad brakes, and all the dogs run free. Barking is allowed,
and every pocket holds a treat. Sit. Stay. Good dog.

***

"Retriever" was original published in *Barbara Crooker: Selected Poems*, published by FutureCycle Press, 2015.

For Rupert

Veronica Lac

You thundered past me
in a whirling black cloud of feathered fetlocks,
as the sand you kicked up
danced like stardust in front of my face
Wind-whipped mane flying behind you -
A vision.
I, forever changed.

Memories of hazy, lazy, summer days
My lips on soft muzzle,
wiry whiskers on my nose, warm breath shared
Inhaling your sweet aroma, exhaling my fears.
Asleep in the grassy paddock lying by my side,
An invisible thread connecting your heart to mine
Following, leading, together,
beauty defined

I went out to the herd calling your name
Pouring out my fears so they'd relay
My message to you
Help me, I said, to fathom how to love another
and not betray
That night you came to me in a dream
I buried my face in your mane
crying tears of joy, feeling your breath on my face.
I was home, again.

You gazed deep into my eyes,
then nudged my back
pushing me towards the herd
Panic gripped me, a gut-wrenching pain
"There are others waiting" you whispered, "It's okay"
Slowly I walked towards the herd
I turn, you stayed

Waking, I knew the lesson you gave
was to love with abandon

without preparing to grieve
That my heart holds eternally
all that we've lived
the rhythmic hoofbeats of my Goth-rock pony
seared into my soul, forever remain
For all that is impermanent, one truth holds
Forevermore, I will never walk alone.

Photograph by Kien Quan Lac

Ashley at Eighteen

Dave Morehouse

When night slams down, like the door
to the garage that's finally fixed,
darkness drives loneliness
across the lap where you sat

and—near the end—
simply slept,
I miss you

and yet

friends snort
at missing a cat.

For Her, With Gratitude

Elizabeth Kerlikowske

Only fifty-five years since I'd put my arms around a great big dog, a muscle taut with energy and strength, yet willing to sit and be clung to, patient as the seasons. My body remembers, when I embrace a friend's dog, my childhood dog, a boxer I could hug and lean on. Our guardians didn't want a dog, but we'd all been through so much, they took her when they took us. All she wanted was to be in bed with me during thunderstorms and run the fields with our neighbor dog. She never caught tadpoles in the shallows but didn't stop trying, the last piece of my real life with parents which made her more than a dog; everything lost still lived as long as she did. And on the morning she did not, I was comfortless.

Goose Bumps

Ellaraine Lockie

The two Easter goslings grew
Too wild for an unfenced garden
in a town with cars and truck traffic
Too big for their wire cage
Where they stayed
when I couldn't stand guard

I heard on the radio
how full-grown geese
would give back that safeguarding
Would protect their people and their place
But that place wasn't meant to be mine

Because my uncle bundled the geese
in the back of his pick-up
Said he'd keep them for me
out on the farm
Would keep their names too
Audie Murphy and Gene Autry
(Our town just got a movie theater)

Said he'd fatten them up
Then he smiled at my dad
There was something not right
about that smile
The same smile confusing his face
at Thanksgiving on the farm
While we sat around the table
that served roast goose instead of turkey

Be a big girl they all said
A little ranch woman already at eight
My first dose of real ranch-life medicine
I didn't swallow it
Nor Audie and Gene
I didn't forgive my uncle either

each time he told the story all those years
Wearing that smirky smile

When the uncle's love-of-his-life
second wife died
I held his hand, played cards
Drove him places
He told the geese story
This time he didn't smile
And I hadn't become that ranch wife

***

First published in the Silver Birch Press "Me, During the Holidays" Series, Dec. 21, 2015. Reprinted with permission.

Sunny

Nance L. Reynolds

Tuesdays. they did come and go,
often predictable like a tweed coat,
patterns lending comfort, yet going nowhere memorable
a subtle sameness, like a unified garment.

No sleeves or collars missing, buttons in place.
No bachelor button in the lapel.

One Tuesday in late November was not the same.
Every little thing was different, but I did stay with the patterns,
it took much and great will,
just to feel the subtle comfort of the tweed.
Because every little thing was different... on this Tuesday.

We took our morning walk, you and I
through wet, autumn leaves... green gold red brown
all mingled and staining one another.

My girl—you paused.
there was nothing to pause about—
no critter scurrying,
not even an old tennis ball, or beyond any of these things...
no broom.
The pause haunted me as your gait lingered.
where was your zest? the way you met each day, every day.
I desperately threw the ball
and then the dread nearly drowned me.

Through my great will, I kept this secret at bay.
We sauntered home together you and I...
as I tucked the great fear away, in pockets of tweed
feeling just to be sure the buttons were in place.
I knew.
Yet each moment my great will exerted such force of optimism
....crushing optimism.

I reminisced lying next to you
in the bitter cold, that icy winter night.

Me shaking with grief, of another ending,
You placing your paw on my arm—whispered your care.
Me scared.
You healthy, aging yes, but full of life...

Let me see here... dog years times seven.
The warmth of your cozy, soft dog-smell body next to mine-
we spooned.
From deep within my shaking body came a plea,
Joining with tightly woven corners of fear in my mind.
I prayed to you, like a child to a god
and this is what was said...
please don't you leave me too.. give me one more year,
"Sunny. give me one more year I prayed "

Fear, hiding again as I ritualistically leave for work.
bidding you goodbye just for the day
I notice a drop of bright red blood from your soft, beautiful nostril.
the world stopped.

Tuesday is not the same. All threads unraveled.
watching listening feeling your breath
fear is here death is here demanding to be known—
refusing to be tucked or buried, into pockets of tweed.
It has swallowed me, and you are taking care of me now.
With your eyes and the language of your body,
so intimately known to me.

I wished as hard as I could, really hard...
that Tuesday had never come.
Days have their stories.
One turns to the other, and the story with it.

Thanksgiving arrived. Family and friends.
You took your place under the table.
You always knew just when to come out from your small,
under-table cave
of yummy smells legs feet laughter.

Foraging begins.
All delicious bits of the feast are now yours.

All the time... I know. I wish and keep on wishing, as hard as I can.
the hardness of my wishing is exhausting
Tuesday turned to Wednesday... then Thursday
each day there is no place to turn—north, northeast, south, west, southeast...
There just is no place to turn.

We all light candles of hope, yet the hope is hidden far far away.
Deep in the caverns of my furiously beating heart
the four chambers don't even feel unified...
where are the subtle, comforting patterns?
blood flow is choreographed by piercing, screaming fear-
but I can't scream.
All is trapped. Hope evaporates.. like the mist in the morning
it is gone.
very cold.

Only you exist nothing else
Turning and Tuesdays, unified tweed coats all gone-
The world has become this one hour with you.
You quiver and convulse, my gentle giant cannot find peace, north, south, east or west. Directionless. Friday.
We all tremble, weep, frantically try to comfort you...
we cannot find a way.

Rushing to a darkened, quiet room –
on a table now you lie groundless.
It is late at night and I hear the words,
"just let us know when you are ready..."
we wait. our son on the way...
we clutch we grasp we breathe we weep
then we pray talk tell stories clutch.... weep forever,
desperation is turning to the deepest ache I know.

You Sunny... Our golden, golden retriever, our Bodhisattva.
The love of our lives.
You leave us.

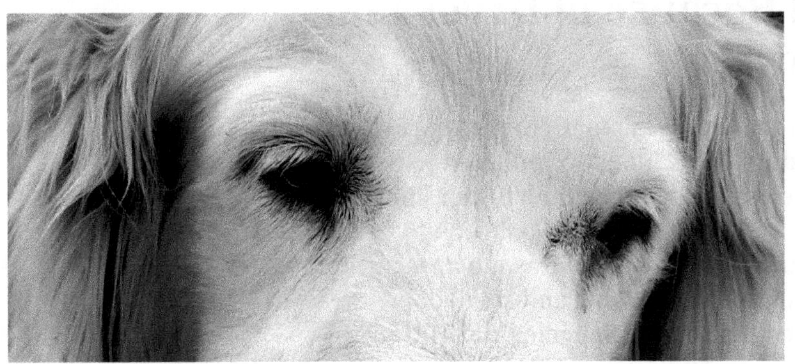

Photograph by Sherri Goldstein

All Because of Dryer Lint

Laurie Kolp

a paramedic gives mouth to mouth resuscitation
to a dog whose lungs are polluted with smoke, one of 67
homeless dogs hoping for a better life

lost mutts who need love as much as purebreds
68 dogs of all sizes, big and small dogs
named Biscuit and Snuggles and Mitten

black dogs, white dogs, spotted dogs, mixed
up together dogs— cockapoos and labradoodles
69 abandoned dogs found on streets with people

who can't pause long enough for pets. They dodge
dogs dumped under bridges and beside IH-10
drivers with cells to ear honking at them

as if they were squirrels, not 70 dogs chasing birds
through the rice fields or fraternizing on Route 71
dogs hidden in bluebonnet clumps, Indian paintbrush

living moment to moment, newborn puppies suckling nipples
in middle of Mom, day-old newspaper underneath them, bold
headlines: road closures along the Texas/Louisiana border

and traffic jammed—not to watch the dogs— but to wait
for floodwater to recede—O, the irony!— 72
caged dogs lined up like prisoners

except they have no voice. Fumes
begin to fill the room, glass shatters, walls
char, 73 dogs alarmed, sirens blare somewhere

faraway, near, mesmeric flames, dogs can't
even catch their breath, 74 innocent dogs
put to death.

In Quest of Life

Mel Goldberg

I set the box
containing the ashes
of my Bichon, Max,
next to me
as I dug the grave
in my yard
to bury him
along with my memories.
Shedding tears for
my pain and emptiness,
my understanding of death.
I smiled and chose a memory to keep.
He always hoped to catch
a lizard, and often dislodged rocks
to find the quick reptiles.
When I told him they were too fast,
Max looked at me
with his dancing eyes
and cocked his head as if to say
I did not understand.
Only the quest has meaning.

Our Angel

Sofia L. Taylor

To Coco, Nov 4, 2001 – Nov 5, 2015

It was love at first sight.
I saw you through your window
and asked if I could hold you.
Once I had you in my arms,
you were mine to keep.
A three-month-old chocolate Labrador,
my first born and soul companion.
You made my house a home
and stole our hearts with no return.
You were the glue that tied us together
and left a hole in us forever.
Dad, Pablo, and I loved you dearest
and you even won mother over.
We all agreed there never was
or will be, another pet like you.
We cherished you for fourteen years,
a true blessing to warm our hearts.
Rest in peace beloved Coco.

Photograph by Sofia L. Taylor

Spareribs in Heaven

Sheryl Clough

for Starbuck

Some people do not believe
dogs are admitted to heaven.
They tell friends whose dogs have died
Just get another one.

Have they never known the soft
paw shoved into a forearm—
one degree of pressure for hunger,
a lighter push for play?

He taught me how to speak without words.
Our syllables soared in silence, all speech
formed of thought waves, our melded minds
fixed on their objects:

the trillium-lined hiking trail,
the deep red cedar woods,
the beckoning graveled beach.

One year ago, near-useless trembling legs
crumbled under him. One year ago, I watched
the needle push its poison. I took a sparerib bone from
my pocket; heard his last crunch, the still-healthy teeth.

Wood floors so quiet now, no click clack
of toenails, no panting slurp in the water dish.
Small sounds that measured our time together
are now high-flying birds on silent wings.

If there is parity in heaven, there will be sparerib
trees sprouting from the clouds, golden and gleaming
as any harp. Until I meet my old dog there,
this chipped bowl of pale lilacs must make do.

Photograph by Sheryl Clough

A Dog's Life

Tom Greening

In the 1940 photo of a dog and his boy
I am the dog.
Somehow, when he died a year later
I lived on as the boy,
although not really.
I died back then
and ever since have been pretending
to be some kind of human.
Most people don't know this about me,
which is OK, because
I've enjoyed parts of this life
even though it's not as good
as the one I had as a dog.

Shade

Tiel Aisha Ansari

Now she inhabits the same space
as the maple that died of root rot
in the year the rain refused to end.

Its leaves were huge, phantasmagorical
and their absence throws sunlight
across the yard in big patches

in which she curls up to sleep. The sound
of the breeze through those immense
palmate greens is the wheeze

of her breath in the last days. We felled
the dead trunk in sections for safety
and they hit the sodden ground

with a soft thump like the sound of her
curling against our bedroom door
ignoring the couch every night

even when winter froze aging joints.
Now she inhabits the same nameless space
as the dead felled tree and lost leaves.

Ready

Laura Gamble

You'll know when she's ready,
the vet said,
Look into her eyes, she'll tell you.
For the next week I slept on the floor beside her,
not wanting to see the look that said.
Let me go.
I wanted to see her ready to play,
tail-wagging joy with Frisbee.
I wanted to see her defiance,
that fierce green-eyed glare
as she knocked books off the shelf,
instead of sleeping the day away.
Did she dream?
And when she looked at me,
her gaze turned inward,
I let her go

Elegy for Keely

Joe Amaral

It's been one week.
I almost forgot
until tonight,
when I watched stars
begin peeking out the
departing sun's bruised eyelid
into a light-swallowed
purple sky
where my shadow
was lost for good.

One week ago I killed
my best friend of twelve years
and I feel as if I drank gasoline
and dropped a lighted match
into my fractured heart.

Soon I'll forget your birthday
like those of my own family
and it burns because distraction
is the enemy of nonjudgmental love.

Twelve years I went from a college drunk
with a puppy
and a morass of responsibility

to a new career
to failed relationships
to various countries and continents
to marriage and kids and owning houses
to changing friendships
to droll stability
to wilting age

and all I have here is a shopping list
to crumple up and throw away
because you were my only true possession.

Preplanning was the worst:
calling the vet
to make an appointment for death,
digging a hole in the open space
between two gnarled oak trees
overlooking the valley
in my backyard
where my neighbors couldn't see.

Did you know? Or was pain your entire being?

You sat there at the fence,
watching me dig
in the sepia afternoon light
where angel-white luna moths
fluttered like tiny snowflakes
as the earth moved screaming
like living skin under my piercing shovel.

I tried to rehash our memorable history, telling
stories through underwater tears you licked clean.

At sunset we went out for double cheeseburgers,
shared them at the beach, the sand a thin strip
pressing our backs against that inevitable cliff.
The fated tide was in and you couldn't run
like you used to, limping along, the chain of my burden
pulling me asea, paralyzing me until morning.

I wanted to keep driving with you forever
in irrationality
on one of those endless concrete freeways.

I can't describe the rest—
the injection, your final breath.
I heard the world go on around me
but I was somewhere else.

I carried you home into that grave,
your muscles already stiff
when I gave you that final pet.

Your brown eyes didn't want to close
and I understood that.
Your golden furred body so flaccid
in my faltering arms,

heavier than anything I ever want to hold again.

I know you're gone on a long hike
faraway over the horizon.
The grave marker I stare at is more for me
to-talk-to-nobody to
make my human self feel better.
I know you can hear me wherever I may be.

I'll never get rid of all this dog hair.
I don't want to.

You are woven into my soul Keely-
I buried the best part of me.

Kingpin

Sandy Stark

Vinny the cat took charge of life to own it,
including the cancer bulking up
in his bladder, which on most days
he dealt with so much better than I.

He was the opposite of retreat. He'd lead me
to his dish or hunker by the door in such
an obvious way I'd have to stop, put the car keys
down, stay home. The price of refusal was high.

I can't count the lives he lived past nine.
If he were a mobster, he'd be the one who,
riddled with bullets, dragged himself back
to his own satin-sheeted bed to die.

I have to give him that: he was one helluva
felonious feline, my swaggering, stubborn,
sweet-faced little kingpin, that Vinny
the Mafioso Cat.

***

"Kingpin" was originally published in *The Toolbox Poems* by Sandy Stark published by Finishing Line Press, 2015. Reprinted with permission.

Photograph by Sandy Stark

Epilogue

J.D. Smith

Brindle dead for a year,
her master wakes at six
and goes out,
still walking her.

I Whispered Love

Patricia Frolander

The grave is so very hard to dig,
frozen soil, packed hard with nature's memories.

He watches me,
pain in his eyes meeting mine.
A sob escapes my iron-clad jaw.

I draw his failing body into my lap,
caress his head
before the plunge of needle into the vein
expels the liquid that will stop his dedicated heart.

As he inhales the last sweet scent of air,
I whisper love
for dog and the man he claims his own—
my gift
to my husband who could not bear to say goodbye.

She Took My Exclamation Point

Claire Vogel Camargo

Since Isabella left us one year ago, I cannot find my exclamation point. Before, it darted out onto hand-written notes, accented my emails and Facebook posts. A ghost now, it is unable to stand on its own.

her mastiff face
black mask on apricot tan
wrinkling forehead
she sings to Happy Birthday
cries Somewhere Over the Rainbow

Fine a few hours before, a year ago, suddenly she was pacing, dry heaves wrenching her one hundred sixty pound body. I called a neighbor veterinarian at home who occasionally saw her. But the vet was already asleep that evening, exhausted, not to be awakened. In disbelief, we loaded Isabella into the car—her breath becoming labored along with the retching, saliva foam on her lips as we drove. I petted her, murmuring, "It'll be okay," until reaching the animal emergency hospital. There I raced in to ask for help, then back out.

her body collapsed
on the asphalt parking lot
by my husband's feet
the light of fight in her eyes
to stay with us, burning bright

Techs rolled her in on a stretcher as I hastily filled out paperwork to admit her. Minutes later, a tech ran out to the lobby. The doctor needed a decision within one minute on resuscitation—our baby was crashing. Opening our mouths to discuss, another bulletin. Too late. Her heart had stopped. We rushed back, saw our beloved. The doctor said the endotracheal tube would not go in—some obstruction. *What?*

sobbing "no, no, no"
I begged her "please don't go"
over and over
repeated "I love you"
again and again – and prayed

My head resting on her English Mastiff back, I embraced her atop the cold metal table. Felt my tears flow onto her large, still warm body – carrying my heart. In hindsight, my exclamation point too. The ineffective endotracheal tube hanging out of her soft mouth, now grotesque. A travesty.

a slower drive home
overwhelming emptiness
crying disbelief
if only that vet had come,
a clay imprint of her paw

How could our happiness have been taken so fast? Had she inhaled a foreign object? Had an allergic reaction that an injection could have reversed? Would my EpiPen have saved her? What could I have done —that I didn't? Days, weeks, months passed. Same questions, slowing frequency.

sorrow's gravity
an occasional chuckle
instead of a laugh
Does anyone notice my
missing exclamation point?

An asterisk replaced my exclamation point when necessary. Continues to. Occasionally my finger hits the exclamation point key while typing. I gasp in guilt at using a symbol of *joie de vivre*, immediately delete it. Surmise that my exclamation point—my joy ability—went to heaven with Isabella.

I guess she might use my exclamation point *up there*—to accent her beautiful brown eyes, happy spirit, bark of words. To needle dawdlers along paths lined with blackberry bushes ripe for nibbling. She loved to snag and chomp blackberries through our cyclone fence. To romp away as I tried to catch her.

Perhaps she will send my exclamation point back in a blessing, I've thought. On a new puppy in our house, to fill our heart holes. In gratitude for the love we lavished on her for almost ten years. In fulfillment she feels from her unconditional love of us—her body an ever ready pillow. I'm glad she has that piece of me with her to cradle in sleep or gnaw on in her waking.

chin licks
cold nose and muzzle nuzzles
no more
her face asleep in the frame
atop my chest of drawers

Hungry to cuddle puppies, nine months later we visited a Great Dane litter. Found "Sophie"—black with white chest and paws. Brought her home a month after, thinking she would be similar to a mastiff in temperament. We learned otherwise.

Sophie was the alpha dog of her litter—energy level was/is off the mastiff charts. Her obsession with chewing shoes and furniture, hyper-alertness and responses, inability to stay still for one minute even when comfortable—all new. Her watching the television. The long skinny body and legs. Lying in the corner of the sofa, an attempt to kiss her head might prompt a warning growl. Boundaries. If asleep, trying to move her body trips her alarm. Maybe she will grow out of these sensitive reactions—which Isabella never had.

re-playing, re-crying
Isabella's valiant dying,
my stomach clenches
Can there be as big a love
with Sophie?

Sophie's behavior has been smoothing out a little over the last month, which brings me hope. She's sweet, beautiful, and gives me chin licks. Tired, she lays her paws and head across my lap on the sofa. Once again, I can feel the familiar osmosis of honey-love. Likely the spurt of endorphins or serotonin. Maybe one day I'll call her my therapy dog too. I remind myself to not judge her based on Isabella, and the mastiff breed. That she is a baby.

my exclamation point
still unusable
with its tinge of pain and guilt—

Will my joy capacity
grow with Sophie? Sad, stop?

Writing about Isabella ensures she is not forgotten. I realize now that to focus only on her tortured exit only re-tortures me. But I also don't think that writing about her happy times can cancel it. At least I don't get the palpitations I did the first months after her passing, in the process of writing about her. I can catch myself earlier with a *Stop it** The compulsion to retrace her last hour of agony is lessening. The trying to prove to myself there was nothing else I could have done. To punish myself? To be angry at 'that' veterinarian, who may not have been able to save her anyway.

It's not fair to Sophie, I think now. Or to me. Maybe short-changes us both. I have to believe that I will feel that strength of canine love again. As to when my exclamation point will return, what is the hold-up? I don't think Isabella, with all her love and sweetness, would keep it from me still.

Triptych of a Dog – Birch: Three Poems for Birch

Betsy Snider

I. Early Morning Walk

Frigid air

dogs running
black against white
snow
except
for one small yellow birch
dog
wandering slowly
from side to side
on the road
behind.

II. The Long Goodbye

I watch as Birch
descends slowly
into that long dark night.
She will not return
this time
when I cry for her.
Another voice
calls her home.
I am left
alone
whispering at the door
in vain,
hoping to glimpse
her pale ghost
as she runs,
tail up, ears perched,
toward eternity.

III. Homecoming

I brought Birch home
the other day.

The vet called and left
a message
that the ashes were ready
for me to pick up
at my convenience.

A few days later
I drove into Claremont
to run some errands—
get my new glasses,
buy some groceries
and stop by the vet's.

Simple, really.

Until I picked up
the small square tin
with "Birch Snider"
written on its side.

My heart took
another hit, skipped
a few beats, and my eyes
skittered past the box,
finally rested on the counter
while Joan murmured "sorry."

I walked out, stiffly,
not knowing how to carry
my pain, so visible
and so pedestrian—
a small tin box,
elaborately floral,
with a white label
discretely affixed to its side.

I put Birch on the floor
just behind my seat
where she used to stand,
her breath hot against my ear,
pungent odor of unbrushed teeth
and decaying food wafting
past my nose as she stared
out the window toward
the road ahead.

We drove home together.

Furry Feline, Furry Conscience

Dakota Gundy

Muse, Mystic and furry mate, yellow eyes that pierced your
soul.
She was the inner truths, as well as the mystical truth staring
through me and purring back at me.
She looks deep within and brings to consciousness the inspiration to
write, to just be.
Without a word, thinking about an event that will take place, a
date.
She sat with me and the inner feelings she expressed, acting as my
guide to do the right thing and not go on the date.
I feel it intuitively it is not the right person, but it's just a date.
Guest arrives on time and my furry conscience turns her back
and walks away.
I laugh and humorously say "The date is over because my Furry
Conscience does not approve."
Furry Feline, Furry Conscience was that part of me that judged
my moral code.
With humor she abounded when she did not approve, either pee on
me in the middle of the night, or turn her back to the guest judging
their character, or sitting at the dinner table glaring at the company
and guiding me away from potential bad choices, knowing true love
would find me, but not
tonight.
Furry Feline with love so deep, she helped me develop balance
between independence and solitude, to a time of togetherness
with friends.
She was independent and yet enjoyed social connections with
my good friends
Furry Feline with deep, relaxed and connectedness with the
Universe and herself, she taught me to relax and just be in the
moment.
Diagnosed with feline cancer, even then, no matter the
circumstances she always purred.
Furry Feline, my furry conscience taught me emotionally to fall back
on my feet, be resilient no matter.
Thank you my Furry Feline, Furry Conscience, muse, mystic that was
a guide until the end.

Astro

Marna Broekhoff

Found in a drainage ditch outside Veneta, just seven weeks old
White-tipped tail, white ruff, white cheeks
Yoda-like ears, always on the alert
Soulful eyes, one blue, one brown
Slender white bowlegs
Salt and pepper hair on a coyote-like profile

Grabbing the leash and prancing ahead in his joy at going outside
Cantering beside me in dappled sunlight on the jogging trails in Hendricks Park
Doing his "mad dog routine," racing and barking on the beach or in our yard
Herding all his people on a hike, forward and backward, carrying his own backpack
Standing tall and proud even if the smallest creature on the scene
Leaping into bed with us during sudden thunder storms

Snowshoeing at Gold Lake with his red fleece coat and booties he hated
Escorting me as "best dog" down the path to our wedding ceremony on the Moon Terrace
Marching in the Fourth of July Parade
Celebrating his 17th birthday with balloons, hat, a dozen humans

Cataracts formed, hearing gone, every plant and pebble sniffed on short, labored walks, hourglass figure now skeletal, struggle to stand up, sag downwards, sad look in his eyes telling me he needs to go now, my beautiful, wonderful doggie for 18 years.
Safe journey, Astro.

Empty food bowls, empty bed, leash untouched on the closet hook, unused chair, quiet house
No wet nose, no licking tongue, no joyful bark, no huggable coat, no adoring eyes.

Only deafening silence and holes in our hearts and lives that refuse to be filled.

Photograph by Alex Broekhoff

Bob

Tom Greening

Few things in life are ever better
than owning a Llewellyn Setter.
When I was just a lonely boy
Bob was a constant source of joy.
Now I've grown up and miss him badly
and still remember very sadly
the day he died and childhood ended,
but still I sometimes have pretended
that Bob is home awaiting me,
and blessed with immortality.

Photo rights Tom Greening

Dog

Maura Snell

I know you by your breathing, the scuffle of ins and outs.
I know you by your heavy potato sack drape.

In November when the last of maple leaves cling
to gray and blackened branches

you become a shape-shifter.

On the first anniversary of your death you are the jogger
on the path in the woods behind our house.

I can tell by your gait.
I wait on the screened porch as you go by in case you stop for water.

I leave your bowl out on the stoop.

On the second anniversary of your death you are the politician
at the Stop-n-Shop. You smile and hand out pamphlets.

Your collar is clean, your black hair shines with pomade,
your shoes with polish.

You love your baths and so I appreciate your aftershave.
Do you remember the day you arrived?

We walked together up to the field.
You pulled hard on the leash.

It was winter then, too.
The grasses were brown, buried under cold.

I let you run from fence post to fence post.
You searched for escape.

On the third anniversary of your death
you are the commuter train. You rumble by hourly.

I'm shocked at your tenacity, your ever-calm timeliness,
all the souls you carry along your way.

Not once do you veer from your course to chase a squirrel or rabbit.
I'm so proud.

This year you are the wind.

You tap dance through leaves shocked with color.
I know it's all subterfuge—you will not come inside.

I leave the door ajar.

I can hear your nails click on the sidewalk,
your soft moan, your recalcitrant sigh.

Just a Dog

Lisa Vallejos

They say, "it's only a dog"
I wonder if they have ever
Had "only a dog"
Like mine

Her name is Dori
I brought her home
When she was left to survive
On a ranch in Texas

She has lived with me in
Four states
Through two
Pregnancies

She curled around my bulging womb
her heartbeat and warmth
comforting me through the hardest
times of life

Dori looks at me
With her sometimes tired eyes
Her hair is turning grey
Her movements slower

I wonder how much time
Remains in her hourglass
How many more times I'll
Be greeted by her wagging tail

I tell myself not to think of it
I know I must
Be prepared for the inevitable
That seems to be lurking closer daily

When that final, awful day comes
I hope to be with her

Holding her closely and wrapping her with
The love she has gifted me

I'm not ready—I'll never be
Prepared to enter my home
Without her hiding under the covers
In my bed

Now, I hug her often until she
Wiggles away
Sometimes tears burn my eyes
I beg death to stay its hand

She is always here—my ally
My closest friend
The warm being whose fur has
Caught countless tears

She is not "only a dog"
She is my family
She is my friend
I love her

She's still with me today
But she won't be forever
Her years are adding up
Much faster than I like

Today, I hold her
I rub her belly in just the way she likes
Now, it's my turn to curl around her
To warm her with the love she's given

And deserves.

At Polly's Grave

Marilyn Flower

First visit after her burial

There was one pale
blue flower still alive,
not blooming but alive.
My heart had said "blue"
when I bought the bouquet
for your grave. Dianne
chose the flowers—I couldn't.
"Feminine" suggested
the florist but I said "blue."
And there it was, blue,
waiting, the one flower
from the old bouquet
that was still alive.

Polly, you got me down
to Orange County,
lived through three terrible
months at Trish's with awful
crazy Keisha the Big Dog.
The rage Trish had
inside her was scary
but you loved us both
through all those terrible times.
That Wednesday night,
before you ran into traffic
searching for her, I called
my home phone from New York,
hoping she was there
at my apartment.
Later she told me she hadn't
come to see you that day.
Oh how I wished the answer phone
were on so I could talk to you,
so you wouldn't be lonely.
That's why I called, to tell

her to switch it on
so I could talk to you.
I felt your abandonment.
I called her house, too,
gave up when she didn't answer,
scolding myself that I was silly,
comforting myself I'd be home
with you in just two days.

I saw your tumors as you
lay on the mortician's table,
crushed, so small.
There were so many
in your stomach, Polly.
How had I managed
not to see them,
not to feel them when
I picked you up and held
you all those days?
Were you in pain, dear little dog?
Had you been staying just for me?

Artemis and Sophia at the Water's Edge

Gina Belton

Cherished companion
Summers on the river bank
Warm haunch, my pillow

Tearing through forests
Early morning redwood runs
Our vitality joined

Like Artemis and
Her kin in the wild places
Together we journeyed

I called you Sophie
You graciously consented
Deep soul of brown eyes

An ordinary day
Black Lab, joyful play, lagoon
Algae bloom choked you.

Terrible poison
Hidden in the water's edge
A place you knew well

You slipped away in
My embrace, tender and sure
Deep soul of brown eyes

I called you Sophie
Goddess of wisdom, the dove
Your true heart, in mine

Hidden in the water's edge.

When Love Walked In On Four

Annette Hope Billings

He arrived a feisty mixed-breed pup,
who woofed gleefully through my front door,
I had no idea how he'd impact my life
when love walked in on four.

He proceeded to dig and incessantly chew
possessions I had come to adore,
I became the epitome of patience
when love walked in on four.

Over time, my heart became his residence
and I was transformed to my core
by the indelible paw prints on my life
when love walked in on four.

He was companion when life was difficult
and taught my love-wary heart to soar,
he was a constant and benevolent friend,
when love walked in on four.

As hair on both our heads grew gray,
when our youth became a tale of yore,
we walked together into old age
when love walked in on four.

He has now traversed the rainbow bridge,
and sorrowful tears often pour
as I lovingly touch reminders of him,
my friend who walked in on four.

Although his loss brings tremendous grief,
my life would be enormously poor
had I not had the gift of sharing my years
with a love that walked in on four.

Much is made of human love
which I, too, sought furtively before,
but he taught me devotion is only partially known
until received from who walks in on four.

Preparation

Joan Canby

Geordie May 2001 to 2014

First I pick up your dead weight
like my hope you would be enough:
four-legged, matted-black coat, almond-shaped kind eyes.

No cunning, no glittering grandiose self-importance,
confident as the oak tree growing in my shaded, blessed garden.

Perhaps I'll call someone. Who? My grief begins now,
readying myself for a day without tail up, and a morning bark.

Preparing myself as I imagine picking you up, to kiss your forehead.

Then I will call the one to dig the 7-foot deep hole.
I will wrap you in the red Stewart tartan cloth,
once your bed now your shroud.

My burly handyman will come in his truck to dig, as I hold you,
wrap you, and tell you I love you. Then I will watch as the hole
widens.

Then I will put you down into it. Watch again as the earth
covers the red-plaid tartan. Your toys are left in your basket,
forgotten.

Then I will run back and find your favorite white stuffed bear,
your first toy as a 6-week-old puppy.

It is wrapped inside the red cloth with you. I don't cry, yet. I will
watch
some more. It is calm. I am calm. I pray to the angels to take care of
you
until I join you. I never say goodbye. Goodbyes are not for those you
love.

Then we will go inside. It is over. Dressed, covered, and buried.

I will then undress, shower, go to bed too.

Return Home

Sally Showalter

Sterling came home in a pretty bag with
blue tissue paper.
My husband, anxious and shaken, laid
him in his favorite rocking chair, like a
baby going to sleep.

He was asleep, a bed of soft ashes.

I gently lift him in my arms, read his name,
the date of his last breath.
Sterling like silver, of luster, eyes, shades
of blue that swam in shelves of oceans.

I kiss his name and hold him to my lips.

His memory now in a wreath of lipstick, of love
and longing for a pillow of soft cream and
chocolate fur, a vibration of his song.

Sterling came home today...to stay.

Driving Home After Putting Our Dog, Chester, To Sleep

Neil Carpathios

I make up a story for myself,
the way we do
when we say goodbye.

He is underneath God's piano,
howling, as God plays,
the way he always howled
in our living room.
But nobody yells shut up.

He pukes on God's hardwood floors. No one minds.

He comprehends now
why humans brush their teeth,
why they throw their voices back and forth
and stare at a box for hours that lights up.

He finally realizes his name was not his name.

He is unfixed and horny again.
He is never locked in a garage any more.
He gets to dig in any garden.
There are no leashes.

He forgives us the swats on the rump with newspapers,
the *No Dogs Allowed* signs we post,
the breeding of his kind into long-legged,
goofy-looking Afghan Hounds and nasty,
yip-yapping fur balls.
The way we played God.

He sympathizes with things that think they need pets.
He does wonder why we took so long
to stick the long needle into his leg
which floated him on a magic carpet—
to where he doesn't have to hunch down

to shit in a yard any more,
while humans watch and comment
on the size, shape and color
of what comes out of him.

He really hated that.

A Poem About a Dead Cat

Amy Durant

For you, Sinatra

Everyone writes a poem about a dead cat. I mean, it's almost
a rite of passage for poets, especially spinsters with glasses.
Everyone thinks their cat was special, right?

You were stupid, cat. You ran into walls with your head
and hissed at them as if they'd attacked you. You fell
off things. You wandered around the house yowling
looking for me until I told you "I'm right here" even
if you'd been sitting with me five minutes before.
You had a third of a tail and made up for it
with far too many toes, some hanging on like lampreys.

I saved you from some idiots who threw you from
a moving car and patched you up and it took months
for you to come out from under my bed. You were
waiting for it all to go pear-shaped again, cat. Until
one day, you gave up and woke me up with a mighty
headbutt to my face that clicked and clacked my teeth
together. You furry fat behemoth. You silly monster.

You traveled across the state with me, across the
country, sometimes more quietly than others. You
slept on my pillow, but sometimes wandered and ended
up on my head. You snored. You got up on your back
legs and begged for treats like a needy kangaroo. You
trotted after me like a puppy and hid from visitors
as if they were coming to take you away. You were
never sure that this time, this was for keeps.

You got a tumor, you stupid cat. You were only
fifteen. You were supposed to live forever.
You became a skeleton. You could barely eat. But you,
you stupid, stupid cat, you wanted me to hold you, still,
all the time, you wanted to cuddle, you wanted to be

on my lap purring even as you drooled blood and pus
out of your treacherous broken mouth.

Have you ever had to make the decision to kill
something you love? Yeah, you probably have. People's
pets die all the time. It's harder when you live alone. It's
harder when you have no one to go with you, help you
carry your once-hefty cat into the vet's office, listen to
his stupid, stupid purring, know that in fifteen minutes
or so, he's never going to do that again because you,
you, the person who's in charge of taking care of him,
has brought him like a sweet, trusting lamb to slaughter.

I cried all over you, you stupid cat. You looked at me like
I'd lost my mind. You headbutted me even as the vet was
putting the needle into your leg. You were purring so hard
she couldn't hear your heartbeat slow and stop.
And I watched as the realization crossed your eyes it was over.
Your eyes went from safe and half-closed to wide,
scared for a moment, then you were gone; that was it.
I no longer had this very stupid, very warm, very sweet,
very loyal cat in my life. And I wailed.
I wailed like I'd lost my child. I don't know that I've ever made
a noise like that in my life. I could hear myself and there was
a part of me that was judging myself for this and then there
was the other part that was screaming, screaming even louder
that I'd killed the only thing that had ever truly loved me,
that ever would, and what the hell kind of monster did that make me.

Your eyes wouldn't close. I tried and I tried to close them
and they just kept opening. I ran my fingers over your paws.
I smoothed your fur; you always hated it messy. Your tongue
was out. I pushed it in. When the vet came back in with a bag
so I could bring you home for burial, I picked you up.
How much did your soul weigh, you stupid cat? You weighed
nothing now. It was literally impossible that from one moment
to the next you'd lost that much weight.

My father dug a hole and we buried you in the woods, under
a pine tree, next to the tortoiseshell cat I'd had when I got you.
I couldn't look when he put you in the hole. I didn't want to see

you with dirt in your fur. You hated being dirty. You'd have
been so disgusted. I didn't want to know if your eyes were
still open. I didn't want to see you like that, you stupid cat,
you stray aberration that wandered into my life and stuck
there.

At least once a day my bed creaks when I'm nowhere near it.
It's the noise it made when you jumped on it because you were
a fat, fat boy. Big-boned, I'd say, but we both knew you were
a chunky furball. I didn't mind. You were warm and fluffy
and so damned beautiful it hurt to look at you and you were
mine
and I didn't deserve something like you in my broken life.
Usually I believe in ghosts and I'd like to believe it's you
but I can't forgive myself for killing you. I can't forgive myself
for not loving you enough that the sheer dint of my will
didn't keep you alive running into walls and snoring our way
asleep until we're too old to know what's good for us.

I have dreams I've misplaced you, or you've gone to live with
others,
and I've come to bring you home. You're hiding under a bed
and you hear my voice and you run to me so fast your skull
smashes my kneecap; you are fat, happy, you mold yourself
into my side so I will never let you go again. And I wouldn't,
my wonderful, stupid, amazing cat, the most love anyone
has ever known in a fur coat. I'd never let you go. You were
mine
from the moment I saw you limping across the parking lot,
thrown away like trash, and I'd know you anywhere. You were
made just for me, and I've lost you, and still, even now, some
days
I don't think I can survive this, this house without you in it.
The practical voice in my head tells me you were just a cat.
The voice in my heart screams, no, but he was mine.

Photograph by Colleen Miller

The Love of a Childless Mother

Veronica Lac

"You don't know what real love is until you have
a child of your own," she says
as if the love that I feel for those in my life
is inferior to hers for her child.
Not enough to feel less than a woman,
betrayed by my body,
but now even my love is less than?
No, I will not accept that.
A childless woman I may be, but a mother I still am

No, I did not carry my children in my womb
but I hold them in my heart, always
No, I did not endure the pain of labor
but I will protect them with my life
No, I did not suffer sleepless nights
but I hold them in my arms
as they gaze at me with innocent eyes
cherishing each moment, each breath, each sigh.

My children feel the pain of separation
as much as yours,
My children thrive on my love and attention
as much as yours
My children are taught boundaries,
are disciplined when needed
and loved always.
What makes your love more real than mine?

Though mine are not human,
they are sentient souls
with their own unique ways of being in the world
and posses the talent of rendering me transparent
to the core of my being
asking only for authentic meetings
enlivening me, challenging me
to be fully present in relationships,
so that I can be courageous with you

and ask you not to dismiss my love.
For the love of a childless mother
is equally fierce, and
is equally real, and
is worth much more than you'd ever know.

***

"For Love of a Motherless Child" was original published in *Capturing Shadows: Poetic Encounters Along the Path of Grief and Loss* by Louis Hoffman and Michael Moats. Published by University Professors Press, 2015.

After Seventeen Years

Robin Michel

This is a poem for my cat, Pudder.
After seventeen years, I have finally learned
how to sleep with you purring in the same room.

I have fed you and changed your water,
cleaned out your litter box, and once attempted
to rescue you from a house being flea-bombed
only to find you sitting beneath a tree, silently watching
as I came out empty-handed and coughing.

But I seldom played with you, or held you in my lap,
and only carried you when I needed to take you to the vet
or wanted to put you in the laundry room so that I could sleep
without you scratching at my door during the night.
For seventeen years, my bedroom has been off limits.

This morning, as I write you this poem,
the hum-purr of your tiny throbbing body
is the only music I need or desire.

This morning, I woke to hear you in the litter box
placed close to my bed near your makeshift bed
upon towels prepared in case you could not climb in.

I crushed the Prednisone and mixed it with tuna.
After you ate and drank, I stroked your head, tilted it back,
and forced into your mouth the syringe of painkiller.
I listened to you purr.

As I stroked you, I avoided your back.
I did not want to again feel the bones
now visible beneath your fur, did not want to think
of the many diets prescribed for you through the years
or what this new weight loss means.

I avoided your right hip, where the bone is mostly
non-existent and the tumor is not.

How could I have not seen the lump
until the vet pointed it out?

Will you—have you—forgiven me?
What is it you say with the vibrating hum
of your body?

Today I will go to work not knowing if tonight
I will have the gift of being able to hold you,
stroke your fur, and give you the love
I only discovered after seventeen years,
in this, the last days of your long life.

I Killed Amber Today

Jackie Peters

I had to kill my dog today
I know it's not the right thing to say
Is it easier to say I put her to sleep
That isn't better I still sit and weep
I saved her many years ago
Where she came from I do not know
A message was sent she needed a home
Wondering the streets all alone
Her time was up the message said
For tomorrow she would be dead
In a shelter quite far away
I went to get her the very next day
When at first I brought her home
She would hide in the closet all alone
But slowly she came out of her shell
Knew she was home that all was well
I named her Amber because she was red
From the tip of her tail to the top of her head
For many years she was always there
So many things that we would share
But I'm sure as you all know
The time would come when she had to go
I watched her slowly age each day
She could not see but found her way
She could not hear
But felt me near
I kept her here as long as I could
But things were no longer good
last night when I heard her bark
She was outside lost in the dark
I searched until I finally found
Her lying quite still on the ground
I had to lift her up to the top
There she lay limp as a mop

The first thing I did was call the vet
Asked him was it her time yet

Slowly I carried her to the car
His office was not very far
I stayed beside her so she would know
That I was there as I watched her go
I stroked her head and rubbed her ears
Nothing would stop my tears
I know the phrase is put her to sleep
But still I sit and weep
Because no matter what you say
I killed my love Amber today

Dogs Try

Tom Greening

Dogs try to teach us to love
right now.
Then they die too soon
and we forget.
We get another dog
and learn a little more,
but not enough.
We each should wear
one of those collars
through which the dog can administer
a mild electric shock
when we forget.

You Never Asked "Why?"

Michael Moats

Something was missing in my life
That I was needing.
It was that friend who could relate
With whom I would not be competing.

The first day I saw you
In that cage set up high
I knew we belonged together
And you never asked why.

You were found on the street
Alone, dirty, and scared.
It was something in our gaze
That told me our hearts were paired.

You grew as we played
And you watched butterflies in the sky.
Such excitement and wonder
Yet you never asked why.

The chewing, the messes,
And barking at night,
You protected me so well
From that dry leaf taking flight.

Nature's trail awaited
For our daily walk outside.
Sometimes the storm clouds blew in,
Yet you never asked them why.

You walked with such enjoyment
Out there the world seemed right.
New or old, it did not matter
Fragrant scents of varied delight.

You shared your desire to continue
Through the leash pulled tight
But when I said, "Let's go"
You never asked why.

Too often in a hurry
For work or for some friends,
For me the night would pass quickly,
For you the night seemed to have no end.

I quickly swiped your fur
As I hurriedly passed by
You appreciated what you received
And you never asked why.

When I yelled out of anger
I saw sadness in your eyes.
You waited for it to pass
And you never asked why.

A lifetime of love
And today you died
Something you accepted
And I am left asking why.

Why this day?
I'm not ready for you to go.
It is something I must face.
A truth that I know.

A lifetime of examples
on not asking why.
To love while we can
And to enjoy the changing sky.

Too many questions
Will leave little time
To love those that matter.
Tis a pity, tis a crime.

A hole in my heart
A tear in my eye
I'm trying so hard,
Trying hard to not ask why.

Your love given so freely
A dedication to admire
To share with you another day
Is my heart's greatest desire.

You silently crossed over
And the light passed from your eyes.
Knowing I would be left behind
You never asked why.

I know you would have stayed
Had you been able to let it pass by
But you heard the final "Let's go!"
And you never asked why.

Collections

Lessons on Grieving: Poems for Amaya

Louis Hoffman

Photograph by Louis Hoffman

Aging

Louis Hoffman

Amaya, girl
We walked paths today
    We took so many times before
Immersed in your joy, I watch
    Your spirit still so strong, yet
    Aging...
Hampered, you limp through the same stream
    You tromped through as a pup
Your zest now restrained
    By aging body
    No longer knowing which season to shed
Our walks shorter now
    Me, sorrowfully content
    With the last days of your presence
You, content to be in the nature
    You soon will join

I Had to Say Goodbye Tonight

Louis Hoffman

For Amaya

That big ol' moon wasn't quite full
As I drove home tonight
A piece of it was missing

I felt that I was entering a time
Like that of tonight's moon
Without the grace of such brevity
You lay on the mat
Barely able to look up
I knew of your suffering
When even the salt of my tears
Didn't draw your tongue
I knew the decision I did not want to make

In the midst of these many strangers
I felt no shame in my tears
No desire to hold back
I never hid anything from you
And now was not the time

I wasn't ready to say goodbye
As I held your face
Cupped in my hands
I stared in those blue eyes a last time
I wouldn't look away
So the face that loved you so deeply
May journey with you from that last breath
Then they were your eyes no more

Sitting with you on the floor
At times I thought I saw a breath
I knew... I knew...

My walk felt as unsteady as yours a few hours ago
As I walked to my truck in that peaceful night
That held no peace for me

Back home it felt so silent
Though the noise was no different
Than the night before
That relaxed phase of crying settled in
As memories bearing the grieving process
Carried you still with me
But each time I realized
There would be no more memories
A jolt set more tears free
With gasp for air as if reaching for you
You were always my comforter

So many times I heard you were just a dog
But tonight more than ever
I wanted you to know
I never believed that lie
And tonight, as I held your face
Through that last breath
I never wanted to say goodbye

***

"I Had to Say Goodbye Tonight" was previously published in *Capturing Shadows: Poetic Encounters Along the Path of Grief and Loss* by Louis Hoffman and Michael Moats. Published by University Professors Press, 2015.

Even into Death

Louis Hoffman

for Amaya

Peacefully we awoke to the day...
to your last day

You lay outside
The sun providing you its warmth
The tree its shade
I came outside for our daily ritual
You raised your head to return the greeting
Yet your old muscles could not sustain
As you attempted to answer my call
Fear set in
As I helped your old body to its feet
Unsteady, you tried to follow
But could not

I carried you to the truck
And carried you to the doctor
Then held you in my arms as we waited
I could not leave you to the floor
They took you from me
And they took your blood
Anxiously, I paced
The night was so calm
But I would not accept its peace

As the news came I resisted every way
I fought the emotions
And challenged the choices
As if to keep you from death
Yet, death will have its way
And slowly I conceded

You came to me carried on a mat
White coats gave us our final moments together
Then returned not so innocent

I held your face and I held your gaze
I remembered my amazement in our years together
You trusted so completely and did not flinch
As my feet danced around you
Grazing your hair, inches from your face
Neither did you flinch or avert your gaze
As I held your face and held your eyes
You trusted me completely
Even into death

Photograph by Lynn Hoffman

A Year

Louis Hoffman

A year came and went
and my hand still instinctively reaches
to scratch your head
Your collar often lies on my desk
or clumsily wraps my hands
the days I choose to write
but all that is left
are memories and ashes
and a fading feeling of your presence

I still have not learned to live without you
My heart longs for watchful eyes when I walk
Your gentle nudge when I am alone
Your tongue when I cry

A Visit

Louis Hoffman

Last night you came to me in a dream
Younger than our last meeting
Standing close
Your fur, soft
Eyes, peering blue
Calmly nuzzling me
Making sure I felt your presence
I embraced you
The touch so real
Even in the dream
I knew the visit was not for long
And treasured the few moments
Though missing you yet, and knowing
I would miss you once again
All I felt
Was comfort and appreciation
You were with me
I felt it
I knew it

Reason tells me
It was just my psyche's need
or some symbolic processing
My heart wants to believe
It was really you
I don't know; I can't know
Maybe
I shouldn't care

Real or illusion,
A dream or a visit
I felt you with me
I felt you
For a moment, again,
You were not dead

I held you while you comforted me
Just like before, whenever I needed you
You were there
And I needed you again

Real or illusion
Dream or a visit
I am thankful.
And thankfully
I am still
Missing you

Something in Those Blue Eyes

Louis Hoffman

For Amaya

there was always
Something
in those
peering blue eyes
Something wise,
silently observing
Something insightful
I often heard people say
you could see right through
to their soul
and they were afraid
but not me
there was just
Something
Something wild
Something beyond

they'd scoff
when I said
you were part of my
Spirituality
but there was Something
in those
blue eyes
where I saw God
felt God
knew God
Something that showed
the wildness of
nature
the vastness of this
universe
not Something to be
controlled
understood

tamed
there was just Something

now that you're
gone
I struggle
to find God
it's not that you're gone
but that you're
not here
not with me
not showing me
and I can't find the way
anymore
but I keep trying
remembering that Something
in those
blue eyes
you'd want that
you cared when I was sad
but liked when I found peace.
in those blue eyes
I could see that

Yet
there's still Something
in those
blue eyes
no longer
with me

***

Originally published in *Journey of the Wounded Soul: Poetic Companions for Spiritual Struggles* by Louis Hoffman and Steve Fehl. Published by University Professors Press, 2016.

Still Missing You

Louis Hoffman

For Amaya

It has been two years now
Since that night I watched
Your eyes leave me

You were so much like me
I, your pack
You, my family
And we both took that seriously
When I took you to the kennel
You'd always fight
I knew what you were saying
You were my home, too
And the days wouldn't be the same
While apart
But that night you didn't fight
Accepting your fate
More gracefully than me

Though family, you were
also more.
Fiercely independent.
And I knew
Looking in those eyes
You were never my dog
Not in that way
You could not, would not
Be a possession
You fought to be something more
And you won
Our family, our pack
Was inseparable

These days, still
I need you
Your ashes upon my shelf

A little shrine surrounded by
Dead pages of scholars and poets
Our picture, your collar, your last
Paw print
Some may make fun, but
Love endures such things
And today, like many days
I sit to write, to change the world
Like I did when you
Would sit at my side
Blue eyes watching
Always with me
I hold your collar typing
More clumsily, but
More inspired, too
And still missing you

Photograph by Louis Hoffman

Distance Encounter

Louis Hoffman

Your eyes fall upon me
I should be scared
but cannot find any fear...

There is something familiar in your eyes,
and I feel safe

You watch as I move among the trees
Standing firm in staring pose
I want to come close
but reason prevents me

Squatting down, shoulders softly angled
I return the intense stare from your eyes
They are brown, not the familiar blue
Yet, something in their presence
Says it is you

"Amaya?"
Softly, I speak
"Is that you?"
Your stare remains firm
And I, unafraid

I want to come close
Yet hold my distance
I feel you calling with your wolf eyes
As Amaya so often did with hers

I lean back into a tree
sinking to the cold ground as
rough bark scratches my back,
still holding your gaze
You lay, head on paws
With loving stare
'I should go,' I think

But cannot leave this comfort
Of you returning to me

I pull my jacket tight
As the crisp night settles around us
The wild night with all its strange sounds surrounds
But I know you will protect me... your pack
And I sleep a needed sleep
Finding a calm I've been aching for

In the crisp morning I awake
Noticing fresh paw prints
and matted grass next to me
Briefly, you are there
In the distance again
Eyes still on me
Then you run off into the trees
In the distance, you turn back
One more long gaze
As your new pack walks up

Walking to my truck
Snow gently blankets the ground
As I ponder my foolish night
Seeking reconnection in the cold woods
"It couldn't have been her"
Then, in the distance
I hear a familiar howl
Tears bind joy with sadness
It no longer matters

Reflections on Poems for Amaya

Louis Hoffman

For many years I have been traveling regularly to China to engage in dialogues and offer trainings on existential psychology. In these trainings, as in my teaching in the Unites States, I often used examples of Amaya to illustrate important aspects of psychotherapy. On my last trip to China before Amaya's death, a person came up to me and said, "Your dog is becoming famous in China." This surprised me, leading me to reflect more deeply about the impact Amaya had on my life. I knew I loved her more than I thought I could ever love a dog, but hearing these words deepened my appreciation for her impact upon me.

I returned home and later that year Amaya passed away. The night of her death the poem, "I Had to Say Goodbye Tonight," began forming while driving home from the emergency clinic where she was given the injection that ended her suffering and took her from me. The tears flowed freely during that drive. I arrived home and my family was asleep while I feverishly wrote the poem. When the poem was finished, I immediately felt a powerful shift in my emotions. It was not the end of grieving–it is still far from done–but I was beginning to accept the pain. It was the beginning of the recognition that the pain was connected to the love and appreciation that I still cherish.

That night I sent the poem to a few close friends—Tom Greening, Dave Elkins, Brittany Garrett-Bowser, Xuefu Wang, and Mark Yang—who knew how much Amaya meant to me. Although these friends were spread across the United States and China, in their responses I felt their love and concern for me. I could have sent a descriptive email telling of the loss and my pain; however, it would not have been the same. One friend, Mark Yang, responded with, "You have to read the poem next year when you come to China." I was terrified at reading these words. I was terrified because I knew he was right, and because I did not know if I could do it. At that time, it was impossible to read the poem without being interrupted by crying.

When the time came, I did read the poem as part of a keynote address at the Second International Conference on Existential Psychology. It was beautifully translated by someone who was herself a psychologist and a poet. As I held in my tears for the talk and the poem, many shared their tears with me in listening, and then in speaking with me afterwards.

After the conference, as we took the train to another city, my ticket was on a different train car from the rest of our group. I sat and wrote "Even into Death." In reading these poems, you may notice the similar themes and phrasing, but there are some important nuances of change, too. Often these subtle changes make a big impact. In "I Had to Say Goodbye Tonight," written the night of Amaya's death, I wrote:

> As I walked to my truck in that peaceful night
> That held no peace for me

In "Even Unto Death," I wrote:

> The night was so calm
> But I would not accept its peace

This is a subtle, but powerful change. As I have supervised therapists in training over the years, I have often heard them complain, "He/she (i.e., the client) is just telling the same story over and over again." Sometimes, this is true. However, often they are not listening for the subtle changes in the story. These small changes, when recognized, are often the big moments in the healing and change process. We need to honor them. Becoming a good therapist or a good listener is often about hearing these small changes.

In the first poem, the night was in control; it held "no peace for me." That night, I felt thrown into the grief. While I knew the end of Amaya's life was near, I expected she would live another year, maybe two. In being thrown into grief, I felt overwhelmed. Over the course of that year, I thought of Amaya every day, and every day I missed her. Yet, I began to take a more active role in the grieving process and decided that I never wanted to stop grieving for her. I did not want to revel in the pain, but I knew the pain was inseparable from the love I experienced with her. I could not hold on to the love without holding on to the pain, and the love was worth the pain.

This is a decision made daily. If we choose the avoidance of pain as our guiding principle, then we will also choose to avoid those things that can cause us pain, such as love, friendship, and many other beautiful gifts of living. This paradoxical relationship becomes more evident in death. With Amaya, I knew the beauty and joy she brought to my life was worth all the pain. The poems for Amaya preserve the love and the memories as they preserve the pain. This is the paradox of grieving: that grieving also involves remembering and preserving.

I began preparing for Amaya's death a year before she died with the poem, "Aging." We were in Breckenridge, Colorado—one of our favorite places. She always loved our walks, but she had an extra zest on these mountain trails. As I often did as she grew older, I took a journal with me to write when she needed a break from our walks. On this walk, we approached a stream that I remember her romping through so many times before. This time, however, she tentatively approached the stream. I can still see those steps vividly in my memory as if they just happened yesterday. Immediately I knew what this meant and felt the pain creeping into my awareness. After she enjoyed the stream for a while, we found a bench and I wrote the poem.

When I have presented on poems about Amaya at conferences, I often hesitated to include "Aging." I do not think it is a good poem, and I considered rewriting it or writing a replacement. Yet, I realized that is one of the reasons why it was important to include it. There is a difference between writing a poem for grieving and writing a poem for a literary journal. While writing for a literary journal may produce powerful healing as well, the focus is different. If we want to fully embrace the healing power of poetry, it is important for us to move beyond the judgments and criticalness of our poetry. "Aging," although not a poem I aesthetically appreciate, was an important part of the story of poetry and grieving for Amaya. It was honest and reflects where I was in that moment. While I do not enjoy the poem, I value it as an important part of the grieving process.

Similarly, "A Year" is another poem that I have never been very fond of. As the anniversary of Amaya's death approached, I felt the need to write a poem to continue the grieving. I knew the importance of anniversary dates, and the power of the loss was still palpable. After several forced attempts at a poem with no emotional connection, I pulled Amaya's collar from the shelf and wrapped it around my hand. Although hard to type like this, I started to feel the sadness, and the grieving process resumed. "A Year" again became an important part of the grieving process.

The next four poems all emerged unexpectedly. "A Visit" began as a dream about Amaya, and the poem is a recalling of the dream with some reflections of my experience of it. When I woke from the dream I strongly felt her presence. As I started to rationally look at the dream, the feeling of the presence left. I regretted switching to the rational analysis of the dream, so began writing the poem to re-engage the emotional side of the dream. I still remember writing the last lines of the poem with tears flowing freely:

> Real or illusion
> Dream or a visit
> I am thankful.
> And thankfully
> I am still
> Missing you

I still remember where I was sitting when writing this poem. I remember the lighting in the room, the time of day. I remember the smell of Amaya's collar and the greasy feeling it left on my hand. I remember the tears, and I remember the emotions. The tears were a blending of sadness and joy. While I had taught and written about the importance and power of preserving our grief many times, with these words the lesson continued to deepen and become more personal. As I felt Amaya's presence again, knowing it was wedded with the pain, I felt overwhelming gratitude join the mix of emotions.

"Something in Those Blue Eyes" emerged following a conversation with my wife, Heatherlyn, about spirituality. I told her, "I know it may sound strange, but dogs are an important part of my spirituality." This was something I had never spoken before, or thought about deeply. To a degree, saying it to Heatherlyn was an emerging awareness that came to completion in writing the poem. Consciously, I was not aware of the meaning that emerged in this poem until after I wrote it. As I read through it again, I felt my love and appreciation for Amaya growing even deeper—nearly two years after her death. In the original writing of this poem, the capitalizations were much different than in the final version. As I reflected upon the meaning of the poem, I capitalized each "Something" and removed almost all the other capitalizations. I embraced the spirituality of dogs.

In writing poetry, we often learn from ourselves. It is not just in the initial writing, but in returning to the poems over and over, recognizing the new meanings. Poems are built upon symbols, and symbols often hold multiple meanings. We may not consciously recognize the full meaning of the symbols when first using them, or we may find new meanings in the symbols over time. When we think we have identified *the* meaning of a poem—even our own poem—we have greatly reduced its power. We should remain ever open to emergent meanings.

"Something in Those Blue Eyes" and "Still Missing You" were written around the second anniversary of Amaya's death. Anniversaries of losses are important. I often encourage clients to keep track of these in their calendar and openly embrace them. They can be painful, but also powerful forces to help us continue our grieving journey. They also can bring new insights, as discussed in "Something in Those Blue Eyes."

"Still Missing You" was written with a soft sadness. The poem was mostly a reflective poem. Talking or writing through the things we love about a lost loved one can be an important part of grieving. This often includes grieving for things that were not pleasant when our loved one was alive. Dropping Amaya off at the kennel was a frustrating experience. She hated it, and I hated leaving her there. I would miss her and worry about her the entire time we were apart. Now I miss those difficult experiences. The message of her pulling against the leash as I walked away was a message of love. I miss that.

Everyone seemed to notice Amaya's eyes, and they became a prominent theme throughout the poems. They are mentioned in nearly every poem in this collection, often with different meanings. Amaya had stark blue eyes that, when combined with her intense stare, were hard to ignore. For some, they were frightening, but for me they provided a deep comfort. She communicated so much with her eyes, including learning to use a particular gaze to tell me when her water dish was empty. Once she was gone, there were few things that I longed for more than to be gazed upon by those eyes.

The final poem, "Distance Encounter," was the biggest surprise of the collection. I wrote this after *Our Last Walk* was well underway. I attended the National Association of Poetry Therapy Conference with my friends Michael Moats and Nathaniel Granger. During one of the sessions, we did an experiential writing from an image of an animal. I chose an image of a wolf, thinking that I was going to write about a wolf. Within moments of starting to write the poem took a direction I did not anticipate.

Although I like the poem, there are parts of it that I feel are not finished, and I would guess there will be revisions to this poem even after *Our Last Walk* is published. There are some poems that I recognize early on are important but are works in progress. Some of these poems take years for me to complete. With "Distance Encounter," I hesitated including it in the book because of this, but after sharing it with Michael and receiving his encouragement I decided to include it. "Distance Encounter" reflects the ongoing longing for Amaya's presence and the continued grieving process. This poem was not based on a real event, but rather was pure fantasy. I still see and feel Amaya's presence—not in a metaphysical sense, but in the sense that she is part of the person I have become. I feel her when I am writing, particularly as so many of my poems and writing projects began on our walks. I feel her when I see other dogs with her gentle spirit. I feel her when I see other Siberian Huskies with mannerisms similar to hers. I feel her in the love I experience from others, and the love I have to offer the world. I feel her in me and know that she is part of who I have become as a person. Yes, Amaya, was a dog. But those of us who have loved and been loved deeply by a pet know that there is no such thing as "just a dog" or "just a cat"–and we are thankful that this is so.

Shanthi Collection

Kristen Beau Howard

Photograph by Kristen Beau Howard

Dear Human, Come Play

Kristen Beau Howard

Good morning human, would you like to play?
    Please pardon me if you may, "lick, purr, and a tumble in fur"

Dear human, come play.
Show me your humanly despair, and I will teach you freedom
You do not have to be anything
You do not need to stiffen your heart in question of
    how
    or when
    or why
Let go. Let go of your body into the air
    of nothing
    of everything
    into the cracks of loving what is and what already was.

Because life is wild and free, just watch me
Because I give and receive as if in perfect harmony,
    feeling your belly scratches and delighted by it all,
    welcoming you home in love of you, and all of you
Dear human, let's play.

The time has come for me to say goodbye
    into the meadows of sun,
    where the grass bends in the wind's flow,
    and the ponds reflect a divine shimmer
Do not be afraid to cry
Do not be afraid to fly

Do you remember all that we learned together?
Do you remember how to play?
    to dance?
    to see?
    to spread the seeds of love that are bursting from your
    bones?

You see human, I have not left you
Look up, within, and around

No matter how lonely, the world is always playing,
and when you choose to join, that is where you will always find me
"lick, purr, and a tumble in fur"
Dear human, come play.

Dear Shanthi, I Am Coming Out to Play

Yesterday has drifted into a stiffened heart's beat, asking
how
and when
and why
Dear Shanthi, I think you taught me how to play.

Meanwhile the cries of grief drip in disbelief
Meanwhile the human world goes on
mornings wake now in silence
the hours are spent without your lick, purr, and a tumble in fur
and evenings are fitted in memory
Dear Shanthi, I have forgotten how to play.

But the time has come to remember,
to get up with a lick, purr, and a tumble in fur
as if this human body were free to let go just like you
of everything
of nothing
into the cracks of loving what is and what already was

The mysteries of life are too much to be understood
You are found in the wittiest of places,
sometimes your cat-like movement fits the beat of my body
or lodged between laughter shared
and even when humanly despair meets in eyes colliding
Dear Shanthi, I am coming out to play.

Reflections on Shanthi Poems

Sometimes life presents itself with something new, and you just know. You know that there is no turning back. In an instant you are changed. Shanthi the kitty (Sanskit for *Peace*) did just this. It is as if she chose which human to live alongside. It is as if she chose to leave this Earth when she did, at only two years old. That is the best way I can explain the phenomenon of Shanthi. She was special. All animals are, but she was different. She had a *pep to her step* that created laughter for all who encountered her. She went on hikes and traveled in cars. She greeted all animals including dogs with pure intrigue. Most important, she was persistent in her need to play and to have all those around her playing too. Okay, I know, all animals play. But Shanthi took this as her mission in life.

On July 13, 2012, her need to play, perhaps, also took her life. It was a warm summer night and I had several friends over for a barbecue. She was not allowed to be outside during the evenings. However, she had each of her human friends so excited about her ballet-type moves and jaunts, she disappeared at dusk. She was never seen again.

I spent my next weeks searching for her, yelling in my sleep, and crying in disbelief. "How could you leave me so soon?" I thought. "It's all my fault" I also thought. One morning life presented itself with something new. I had an epiphany. Shanthi was gone from this Earth, but her teachings were not. I began to see her everywhere. I still do. She stamped my heart with the remembrance and importance of play, and that does not go away. Because of her, I am changed. Writing these two poems helped me through the grieving process by allowing me to experience denial, anger, anxiety, and guilt with more awareness. This poetry helped me accept the unacceptable and to realize that play is always available.

My One Constant: Poems for Jonathon

Lylanne Musselman

Photograph by Lylanne Musselman

Unexpected Visitor

Lylanne Musselman

Lovers came and went,
but for eighteen years you graced my lap,
you slept next to me, and followed me
around the house. You didn't care
if the dishes were done, or if
I gained a few pounds, or shed a few tears.
You were there, a purring anchor—
even as your spirit was leaving me.

Jonathon, you came to me
in a dream last night, strong,
healthy and handsome. You
ascended the wooden stairs
coming up out of the basement,
ran into my open arms.
You reveled in my touch, I cried your name –
my one constant.

***

"Unexpected Visitor" was previously published in *Company of Women: New and Selected Poems* by Jayne Marek, Lylanne Musselman, and Mary Sexson, published by Chatter House Press, 2013. Reprinted with permission.

Teddy,

Lylanne Musselman

my little Jonathon clone, how can you be so alike without ever walking the earth at the same time? Jonathon left me at eighteen years old, two days before Christmas in 2007; you came to me at four months old, a week after my birthday in 2011. Did his spirit find a way back to me? I'm not sure I believe in such things, but when I saw that Humane Society photo of you in the Toledo Free Press, I lost my heart to your heart-shaped face, your tabby cat coat, those almond eyes; the line about you getting your name from cuddling with your teddy bear. I thought you'd be scooped up in someone else's arms before I had the chance to come for you. A week and a half passed before I could get life to slow down enough and to prep my other two kitties for your possible arrival. When I called the shelter you were still there. Was it a miracle or a karmic sign? When we first met, you put your little head in the palm of my hand and purred loudly. Back home, you made yourself familiar in my lap. That night you rubbed your tiny head against my cheek over and over again, brushing away my tears.

Sickly Fellow

Lylanne Musselman

When I picked him up
from the Humane Society,
I worried what I'd done –
my older cats so predictable
and now there'd be new kitten antics –
him swinging from curtains, clawing his way
up furniture or knocking over the flat screen TV.

Instead I got this sickly fellow,
who sleeps away the days,
who loves to snuggle but has health issues
expected with older cats, not a seven-month-old.

Now diagnosed with pneumonia,
he's had more meds in three months
than my previous ten cats combined.
How I wish for the worry of shooing my kitten
off of curtains or mending snagged furniture.

Consolations After the Death of My Kitten

Lylanne Musselman

After James Tate's 'Consolations After an Affair'

Chattering at shadows on the ceiling,
my cats run room to room.
They see little Teddy.
As we settle down at night, he visits.
And I can hear peaceful cats purring,
the love that moves me.
I've discovered that I don't need
a lousy spouse, a loan to repay.
I have unfinished paintings
that wait for van Gogh to return.
They know nothing of sangria and Vonnegut.
For them a foggy night in February
is a ghost of an excuse.

***

"Consolations After the Death of My Kitten" was previously published in *Company of Women: New and Selected Poems* by Jayne Marek, Lylanne Musselman, and Mary Sexson, published by Chatter House Press, 2013.

Reflections on My One Constant

Lylanne Musselman

"My One Constant," is a series of four poems that reflect the loss of my beloved cat, Jonathon, who was my pet for 18 years. Even though I knew there would never be another cat like him, I eventually found a cat that reminded me so much of him that I adopted him as a kitten from a local humane shelter. Teddy had been advertised in the paper, and when I saw him I felt a connection—even though I was not able to go see him at the shelter right away because of my teaching schedule. I was amazed when weeks later that he was still at the shelter and available for adoption. I actually felt because of that fact that we were meant to be together.

Once home, Teddy and I did make a connection and all was happy—until he didn't seem to be thriving. I took him to the vet many times, and they finally diagnosed him with the calicivirus or "cat flu." By that time, my other two cats were infected. After a lot of trips to the vet, the older cats started improving, but Teddy was not responding to the antibiotics. I ended up taking him to a different veterinarian that ran a battery of blood tests on him. They sent him home with me, and I was certain that we were going to find the cause and find a cure for him. That night Teddy died in my bed. So, a kitten that reminded me of a cat that I'd grieved for years was the cause for yet more grief.

On a positive note, my two older cats are still alive and well, and in 2012 I adopted another cat, Fiyero, that has some markings similar to Jonathon and Teddy's, but not as striking of a resemblance as those two had to one another. I know that you can never replace a cat with another, as they all have their own "purr-sonalities," but I am partial to brown mackerel tabbies because of these two sweet cats that have been in my life.

Poems about Three Dogs

Christine Holland Cummings

Last Night, All Three Dogs

Christine Holland Cummings

came home. Jack's belly-fur was black with dirt,
like the compost they spread in the back yard, steaming
and stinking vineyard cuttings decomposed,
with the smell of dark wine laid over all.
I held Jack's lower jaw, my fingers in his mouth
finding a gap between the teeth,
like the place where a horse's bit goes.
His face was older, his good solid body, and Riley
fat and full-coated, and Kell
a nimble girl again jumping from bed to floor.
We sat together, the old pack of four, together. I had thought
they were all dead, and now they were not. They had only
gone roaming, been lost, and come home.

What Remains

Christine Holland Cummings

Now is the persimmon moon, when ragged
ribbon light threads itself through
the cloud collage of late November
afternoon. A harvest of orange hangs
naked on its branch,

softening to jelly, spoonable
from the skin of its own heart-shaped bowl.
Squirrels and gophers take over the back yard.
Like phantom limbs, the routines of affection
ache. Found among hydrangea bracts:
Jack's white hair.

12 Ways to Wipe Tears from Your Face

Christine Holland Cummings

Wipe them with knuckles
dug hard against your skin,
or your shirttail.
Wait for the breeze to dry them.
Use lint pulled from the dryer's screen,
full of hair from the one you lost.
Wipe them with the sheet you pulled over your head,
or push your nose against your husband's chest.
Soft as tissue, leaves
from the hazelnut will do the job,
but glass will mark where they pass.
With ashes, with dirt, with tenderness,
with regret.
Your dog is gone; she can't lick them away.

What I Miss

Christine Holland Cummings

The round barrel of her chest. The ribs under her skin. The flat top of her skull,
soft fur napped tight against hard bone. Her feathered tail, wrists, ankles.
The smell of her. Her heart under my hand. I felt it slow, and slow, and slow and
stop.

The way she howled like a coyote child, a greeting, a demand, an all-purpose
conversation starter, an engagement, a connection, a here I am and there you are
and aren't we just grand together comment suitable for any occasion. I miss that
wild voice.

Why didn't I record it? Why didn't I invent a machine that could catch it all, the feel of her coat,
the silky and the curly-rough spots, the sound of her voice, the thirsty slup
slup slup of her tongue going after water in the bowl in the laundry room, her toenails'
click?

Puppy behind me among the redwoods, sturdy small body clambering over tree
limbs and rocks. Dog before me pushing sheep where I asked her to. Old girl
strolling with me on morning and evening walks. Finder of what's hidden, belovèd
companion.

She came to me in a dream and I hugged her tight, felt her warm solid weight
against me, and cried I've missed you, and stroked her soft fur until I knew

it was a dream and I couldn't stop the waking, the slipping away, the awful loss of
her, again.

Reflections on Poems about Three Dogs

Christine Holland Cummings

Between the summer of 2007 and the spring of 2010, all three of my beloved border collies died. Riley lost his back legs through a slow and progressive neurological illness, and we finally had to let him go. Jack was next to go, from prostate cancer, which we did not know he had until his organs began to fail. He was gone two days later, a kind and jolly dog who wanted nothing more than to play fetch for hours and lean his big head against our knees. Last was Kell, my special girl, more like a daughter to me than a dog. She started to lose weight around the time Jack died, and lost her ability to stand because of vestibular syndrome, and I tried too hard to keep her alive, until at last I had to recognize her misery and let her go too.

These poems were written over the first year or two after their deaths, as I tried to reconcile myself to the loss and the void it left in my life. They are purely poems of sorrow, a way of telling myself and others what it was like without their constant presence, and of recalling them too, just for a moment.

Poems for Spencer

Patrick S. Dixon

Photograph by Patrick S. Dixon

Falling

Patrick S. Dixon

Tonight's stroll around the lake
was comfortable, warm and calm.
Four of us—two tailless bipeds
leashed to Ginger and you, took
our time sniffing the start
of sweet-scented summer.

We talked, footsteps in a weave
about you, pausing at the picnic table
when you looked tired. You lay at my feet
in the muggy shade. I scratched your white face,
and thought, *We can do this for a while.*

But when we walked back to the car
I was watching as your leg gave out
and you fell hard onto the crushed gravel
of the path, filling the side of your mouth
with stones. Your legs trembled as you
rose, leaned against me, panted while
I cleaned pebbles from your mouth.

You took a few steps, sighed,
lowered your head and pushed on.
Matching your slow pace, my eyes
big and wet as your tongue,
I did the same.

Driving with the Windows Down

Patrick S. Dixon

The sky was blue, and the trees
were the lime-green
they only have in April,
spring's opening act.

I hurried to get Spencer in the car
for his veterinarian appointment.
Cool air and wind's bluster bent
the treetops—made me look up,
see where the soft roar was coming from.

He's getting old,
said the short man in the white lab coat.
He isn't as coordinated as he once was.
No wonder he's falling. My eighty-year-old
dad did the same.

I wasn't comforted. Spencer panted
and looked away, haunches
on hard linoleum, expression tolerant:
I'll put up with this guy, but don't expect
me to like it, was the message
I got, but the doc didn't seem to.

He looks like a good dog, he placated us,
and I knew the session was about over.
We were relieved to pay
the bill and get out of there,
drive with the windows down,
ears flapping, tongues out, leaning
together, into the wind.

How Do You Resuscitate a Dog?

Patrick S. Dixon

I'd rather have a different doctor, I said
as I made another appointment for Spencer,
my ailing golden-haired friend. The last visit
was unproductive, and a bit demeaning.
I thought perhaps a new expert would see
his balance problems differently. He was limping
more, and my confidence was sliding down the dark tunnel
from concern to worry. I needed help with the landing
if despair was the outcome. *We'll X-ray the shoulder,*
the new doc smiled, *and see if we find anything.* I was
the one who said the word. *My last golden had bone cancer,*
and I got a sympathetic look. *It's common in them,* she answered,
and often shows in the shoulders. We'll see what's there.
I waited a long time outside on another cool and breezy day,
then went in to wait some more in the lobby.

The pleasant, welcoming atmosphere
behind the counter had changed tone. Only one person
was left attending the clients who were sitting, standing,
barking, meowing. The assistants who showed their faces
looked troubled and disappeared quickly. I watched
one man and his dog get turned away until tomorrow.
We were next. Spencer was led back to me with apologies,
We've had an emergency. Can I schedule you for tomorrow? Her face
was dark as she tried to work the computer, and I leaned in.
Is someone in trouble? She nodded. *We've had an emergency.*
Her hands shook, her smock was covered with light yellow hair.

We returned today for the X-ray, and Spencer seemed
pleased to be back despite my apprehensions.
Another doctor read the negatives.
Looks like a bone chip in his shoulder. Maybe some
arthritis broken away. The good news is that it's not cancer.
We should be able to manage the pain with meds until it eases.

I asked again, and was told someone else's Spencer
had reacted badly to routine anesthesia yesterday,
and didn't make it. *How do you resuscitate a dog?*
I wondered, and felt small at my relief
while another walked out with an empty leash
hanging where their friend should be.

Paws on Either Side of the Door

Patrick S. Dixon

Spencer, my golden retriever, my best
four-legged buddy for the past 15 years,
died last Thursday under the cedar tree
out front. His legs, weak for months, were
finally failing. He began to pee himself at night.
We moved him to the garage to sleep, cleaned
the floor each day and bathed him often. I didn't
hear him bark for help that last night, alone
and unable to stand. My sons heard, told me
in the morning, after I found him in a puddle, and—

No, that's not what I want to write about Spencer.
I want to say we found each other at the pound,
where he stood up after we first met, a skinny one-year-old
on hind legs, put his paws on either side of the door to the cage,
looked at me over his shoulder. *Please don't leave me here.*
I didn't. I want to say how I took him on photo trips and walks
to the beach where we discovered how much he loved
chasing through waves; to the off-leash parks where
he ran and ran and ran, but always kept an eye on
me. How he greeted me in the mornings by rushing over
to bury his head in my crotch before I was ready,
or walked into my office to interrupt my writing
with a lean against my leg, how his tail would wag just a little
when he dropped his head in my lap and I stroked his ears
or gave him a massage when his joints began to ache. How he
would follow me from room to room as I passed my day, how
he'd keep watch in the hall, by the door, at the top of the stairs.

I want to own it was my fault, my decision to end his life,
but he wasn't wagging that last day. Though I wasn't ready,
I think he was. God, I hope so. I don't want to think he isn't
here anymore because I made a mistake, made a mistake.

Early Morning

Patrick S. Dixon

Tonight you caught me sitting
in the grass of my dream,
out front, under the cedar
where we used to wrestle.

You'd act tough, roll
on your back, I'd nibble your
ear, barely bearing down,
until you yipped. We'd both
laugh. I'd scratch your belly,
you'd stretch your legs and roll
over with a sigh.

I used to call *Body Slam* when
you'd run up, drop your head
into my lap, heave your 90 pounds
on top of me, wagging and panting.

I wasn't thinking of all this,
I was just under my dream-cedar
in the shade, when I felt the press
of your heavy shoulder on my back.
I knew it was you, come to visit,
to say hello, say *Remember*?

Reflections on the Spencer Poems

Patrick S. Dixon

The poems in this collection reflect the concern and loss I felt as Spencer, my friend and companion of 15 years, began his decline and showed his age by gradually becoming infirm and less and less capable of continuing during the last year of his life. The grieving process for me began when he started falling while on walks, and gradually built as his condition worsened and we repeatedly visited the vet. I felt a tremendous pressure to make the right decision for him when the time came, but struggled to know when that would be, and felt terribly guilty once the moment came and went.

Writing the poems helped me sort out the sadness and remorse I felt during the process of losing him, as well as the terrible responsibility of being the one who made the decision to end his life, and the deep sense of loss I felt afterward. I'm not sure I'll ever be at peace with that part of it, but the last poem in the collection came from a dream that helped me feel somewhat forgiven and loved by one of the best friends I've ever had.

Poems for Ginger

Patrick S. Dixon

Photograph by Patrick S. Dixon

Ginger

Patrick S. Dixon

While you are still here
what do I say to construct
the cup that holds all the love
all the walks, talks, wagging
tongues and tails, the trust
without judgment or memory
of harsh tones, words spoken in anger,
rooted in the belief this would last?
Do I apologize to you for the injustices,
wrong-headedness, mistaken accusations,
missteps? Tears come to remind me of no more
walks around the lake, scratches behind your ears,
wags, licks, rides with you in the rear—view looking out
the back window, or evenings spent napping next to my chair,
my hand on your side, not empty.

Hurts So Good

Patrick S. Dixon

for Ginger

The space next to me
in this room where I spend
most of my days
isn't empty.

There's no hole next to my desk,
no warm spot left on the carpet,
no rhythmic breathing, scratching
of paws chasing dreams.

I haven't heard a panting sigh in weeks
or the clatter of tags against the water bowl.
Hell, I haven't filled it in days,
and it sits by the door, still full.

Your collar caught my eye tonight
asked me to pick it up, give it a sniff,
looked too lost to hold for long,
or was it me, too sad to look in that mirror?

It's only been two weeks today.
You'd think I'd be past this.
You'd almost think
I don't want to be.

Reflections on Ginger Poems

Patrick S. Dixon

Ginger was a gentle, shy soul. She was diagnosed at age 11 with a cancerous mass in her chest after we noticed her going into a rapid decline. It was too close to her heart to operate, and her history of being abused before we got her and her need for love and calm helped us decide not to subject her to chemo and the disruption of her life that would require. We chose to try to keep her comfortable with Prednisone and pain meds as long as it was effective, which lasted a little longer than a month.

We knew her death was near, and as with Spencer, whom we had lost only five months before, we were already grieving and saying our goodbyes to her as she slipped away from us. The first poem was written while she was alive, and the second shortly after she was gone. She had helped us fill the gap Spencer left behind, but when she was gone the house was empty, and I think we felt the grief even more as a result.

A Small Difference

Tom Greening

When my dog and I are gone
no one will remember
how much he and I enjoyed my petting him,
or care how little that affected the universe.
I mention it here, however, hoping
to encourage a few readers anyway
to pet their dogs more
and not give up attempting
to make that very small difference
in human history.

Poetry Activities to Remember and Grieve Your Pet

Activity 1: Tactile Memories
Find something that reminds you of your pet, such as their collar, a favorite toy, bed, or water dish. If you do not have any of these, a picture will also work. Try to engage as many senses as you can in remembering your lost pet. Spend some time with the memories and the emotions they trigger. After this, write a poem trying again to use your senses to evoke symbols, metaphors, sensations, and descriptions.

Activity 2: Poem in Your Pet's Voice
Write a poem in your pet's voice, as if your pet was able to express him/herself. You may consider writing several poems at different points of your pet's life, such as when first joining your life, when aging, and after the pet has died. If you are struggling to put this into poetic form, write it as a letter. After you have written the letter, identify important symbols, images, and memories. Try to draw upon these to turn the letter into a poem.

Activity 3: Response Poem
After you have written a poem or poems in your pet's voice, consider writing a response to your pet in your own voice. You can also begin this as a letter and turn it into a poem.

Activity 4: Perceptions
Write a poem about how others see your relationship with your pet. You could write a poem or poems in their voice, or in your own voice recognizing how others perceive you. If the poem was written in someone else's voice or voices, you can also consider writing a response poem.

Activity 5: Place
For many people, there are special places that one shares with one's pet. For example, the poem "Aging" by Louis Hoffman refers to a special place in the mountains where he and Amaya used to love to go hiking. Return to the special place for you and your pet with a

notebook and pen. Begin reflecting upon your memories and the emotions of this place. Then take note of the images, smells, and even tastes of this special place. As you get in touch with these, begin writing your poem.

Activity 6: Life/Relationship History

Begin this exercise by writing a life and/or relationship history of your pet. Pay particular attention to how your relationship, feelings, and communication changed over time. Although you could write this as a poem, it is likely easier to write this as a narrative. After you have finished the history, review it, paying attention to what stands out to you emotionally. When you encounter the particularly emotional moments of the history, write a poem drawing on that part of your pet's life. For some, it may be helpful to put the history aside for several days or weeks and then review it.

Activity 7: Poems over Time

Write a series of poems over time about the loss of your pet. This can be done over the period of a week, month, several months, or longer. Periodically look back through the poems, noticing themes, changes in your wording, and changes in your emotions. The poems can serve as a history of your grieving process.

Activity 8: Writing and Rewriting a Poem

Begin by identifying a poem you have already written about the loss of your pet or write a fresh one. Set it aside for several days or a week. Keeping a copy of the original poem, make revisions to the poem. Continue doing this for several revisions, keeping each version of the poem. After you have written several revisions, go back through the collection of versions of the poems and notice changes. Spend some time reflecting on the significance of these changes.

Activity 9: Re-reading *Our Last Walk*

Try reading through *Our Last Walk* again by reading one poem a day. After each reading, spend some time reflecting on the poem and how it relates to your own grieving process. Mark the poems that stand out to you and, after finishing re-reading the book, return to the poems that stood out as most significant for you. You may choose to continue to re-read these poems over time or during times when the grief returns. Pay attention to how the poems interact with your own grieving process.

Activity 10: Expanding Your Writing Style

Our Last Walk intentionally has included a range of poetry styles. Different styles of poetry can have a different personal and emotional impact upon people at various times. Review some different styles of poetry from *Our Last Walk* and identify a few that are different from your own typical style of writing poetry—maybe even different from the type of poems you are drawn toward. Try writing a poem in a similar style, and remember to be compassionate with yourself. Poetry need not feel like good writing to be healing. Pay close attention to your emotions as you write different styles of poetry.

***

A number of additional poetry activities that can facilitate the grieving process can be found in the appendix of *Capturing Shadows: Poetic Encounters Along the Path of Grief and Loss* by Louis Hoffman and Michael Moats.

University Professors Press Books
www.universityprofessorspress.com

An Artist's Thought Book: Intriguing Thoughts About the Artistic Process
by Richard Bargdill

Journey of the Wounded Soul: Poetic Companions for Spiritual Struggles
by *Louis Hoffman & Steve Fehl*

Stay Awhile: Poetic Narratives on Multiculturalism and Diversity
by Louis Hoffman & Nathaniel Granger, Jr.

Capturing Shadows: Poetic Encounters Along the Path of Grief & Loss
by Louis Hoffman & Michael Moats

The Polarized Mind: Why It's Killing Us and What We Can Do About It
by Kirk Schneider

Shadows & Light: Theory, Research, & Practice in Transpersonal Psychology (Volumes 1 & 2) by *Francis J. Kaklauskas, Carla J. Clements, Dan Hocoy, & Louis Hoffman*

Psychotherapy's Pilgrim-Poet: The Story Within by *Betsy Hall*

Love Outraged and the Liberation of the Core Self *by Franklin Sollars*

Bare: Psychotherapy Stripped *by Jacqueline Simon Gunn & Carlo DeCarlo*

Humanistic Contributions for Psychology 101: Growth, Choice, and Responsibility *by Richard Bargdill & Rodger Broomé*

The Buddha, the Bike, the Couch, and the Circle: A Festschrift for Dr. Robert Unger *by Michael M. Dow, Francis J. Kaklauskas, & Elizabeth Olson*

About the Editors

Louis Hoffman, PhD, is a faculty member at Saybrook University. *Our Last Walk* is his eleventh book, and his fourth book in the Poetry, Healing, and Growth series. He has also published numerous journal articles and book chapters. He is a past president of the Society for Humanistic Psychology and is currently the president of the Rocky Mountain Humanistic Counseling and Psychological Association. Dr. Hoffman has been recognized as a fellow of the American Psychological Association (APA), the Society for Humanistic Psychology, the Society for the Study of Aesthetics, Creativity, and the Arts, and APA Division 52 (International Psychology). He serves on the board of The Humanitarian Alliance and The Coalition for Compassion and Action as well as on the board of editors for several journals. In addition to his scholarly work, Dr. Hoffman maintains a small private practice in Colorado Springs. He is a husband, father, and avid dog lover residing in the beautiful mountains of Colorado.

Michael Moats, PsyD, is a private-practice clinical psychologist who primarily focuses on grief and trauma. With research interests in cross-cultural investigation of lessons through loss; experience and appreciation for working with hospice clients and their families; daily client engagement; experience with personal loss; as well as being an animal lover (propensity toward dogs), this project was a natural fit. Dr. Moats has also authored book chapters, articles, poems, and another book, *Capturing Shadows*.

Tom Greening, PhD, began writing poetry 70 years ago and has been unable to stop, despite being a busy psychotherapist in the same office for 58 years, editor of the *Journal of Humanistic Psychology* for decades, and professor at Saybrook, Pepperdine, and UCLA. An admirer of rhyming couplets by Shakespeare, Chaucer, Frost, Pope, Ogden Nash, etc., he has also occasionally been caught writing blank verse. A second, enlarged edition of his *Poems For and About Elders* is in press, as is an illustrated collection for children titled *About Some Animals,* endorsed by his dachshund. His collection, *Words Against the Void,* did not fill it, so a second edition is in press.